WRITING IN SOCIOLOGY

BRIEF GUIDES TO WRITING IN THE DISCIPLINES

Edited by
THOMAS DEANS, *University of Connecticut*
MYA POE, *Northeast University*

Although writing-intensive courses across the disciplines are now common at many colleges and universities, few books meet the precise needs of those offerings. These books do. Compact, candid, and practical, the *Brief Guides to Writing in the Disciplines* deliver experience-tested lessons and essential writing resources for those navigating fields ranging from Biology and Engineering to Music and Political Science.

Authored by experts in the field who also have knack for teaching, these books introduce students to discipline-specific writing habits that seem natural to insiders but still register as opaque to those new to a major or to specialized research. Each volume offers key writing strategies backed by crisp explanations and examples; each anticipates the missteps that even bright newcomers to a specialized discourse typically make; and each addresses the irksome details that faculty get tired of marking up in student papers.

For faculty accustomed to teaching their own subject matter but not writing, these books provide a handy vocabulary for communicating what good academic writing is and how to achieve it. Most of us learn to write through trial and error, often over many years, but struggle to impart those habits of thinking and writing to our students. The *Brief Guides to Writing in the Disciplines* make both the central lessons and the field-specific subtleties of writing explicit and accessible.

These versatile books will be immediately useful for writing-intensive courses but should also prove an ongoing resource for students as they move through more advanced courses, on to capstone research experiences, and even into their graduate studies and careers.

OTHER AVAILABLE TITLES IN THIS SERIES INCLUDE THE FOLLOWING:

Writing in Anthropology: *A Brief Guide*

Shan-Estelle Brown
(ISBN: 9780199381319)

Writing in Engineering: *A Brief Guide*

Robert Irish
(ISBN: 9780199343553)

Writing in Political Science: *A Brief Guide*

Mika LaVaque-Manty and Danielle LaVaque-Manty
(ISBN: 9780190203931)

Writing in Nursing: *A Brief Guide*

Thomas Lawrence Long and Cheryl Tatano Beck
(ISBN: 9780190202231)

Writing in Biology: *A Brief Guide*

Leslie Ann Roldan and Mary-Lou Pardue
(ISBN: 9780199342716)

WRITING IN SOCIOLOGY

A BRIEF GUIDE

Cary Moskovitz
Lynn Smith-Lovin

New York   Oxford
Oxford University Press

Oxford University Press is a department of the University of Oxford.
It furthers the University's objective of excellence in research, scholarship,
and education by publishing worldwide. Oxford is a registered trade mark
of Oxford University Press in the UK and certain other countries.

Published in the United States of America by Oxford University Press
198 Madison Avenue, New York, NY 10016, United States of America.

For titles covered by Section 112 of the US Higher Education
Opportunity Act, please visit www.oup.com/us/he for the
latest information about pricing and alternate formats.

Library of Congress Cataloging-in-Publication Data

Names: Moskovitz, Cary, author. | Smith-Lovin, Lynn, author.
Title: Writing in sociology : a brief guide / Cary Moskovitz, Lynn
    Smith-Lovin.
Description: 1 Edition. | New York, NY : Oxford University Press, 2016. |
    Series: Brief guides to writing in the disciplines
Identifiers: LCCN 2016006853 | ISBN 9780190203924
Subjects: LCSH: Sociology--Authorship. | Sociology--Research. |
    Sociology--Study and teaching (Higher)
Classification: LCC HM569 .M67 2016 | DDC 301.072--dc23 LC record available
at https://lccn.loc.gov/2016006853

9 8 7 6 5 4 3 2 1

Printed by LSC Communications, Inc., United States of America

DEDICATION

For Miller. He taught me to cut out the exclamation points, "extraneous quotes" and compound subjects and objects!

—Lynn

For my Mom. Every child should be so lucky.

—Cary

BRIEF TABLE OF CONTENTS

TABLE OF CONTENTS

PREFACE

Whether you are taking undergraduate courses or beginning a graduate program in sociology, we hope this little book will help make writing in sociology less mysterious and more rewarding.

If you are taking sociology courses as electives, you will find plainspoken advice and information to help you make sense of the (often unspoken) expectations of your sociology professors for composing various kinds of school assignments. If you decide to major or minor in sociology (and we hope you will), you will encounter a number of the types of writing assignments that we describe here as you move through the major courses in Chapters 2 and 3. If you are a sociology senior doing a capstone project or a graduate student, Chapters 4, 5, and 6 will help you will make the shift from being a *consumer* of knowledge produced by others to being a *producer* of knowledge yourself. If you are an international student who is new to the US educational system, this book will help you navigate the expectations of sociology as a discipline and our national educational culture simultaneously.

There are already basketfuls of style manuals, methodological texts, advice books for overcoming writer's block, and comprehensive writing books that discuss how to format different types of research. In this short guide, we have attempted to link the thinking and writing dimensions of the research process. We've also tried to describe how many shorter assignments in sociology classes overlap with the skills necessary for a full report of original research.

Chapter 1 discusses the different types of writing that professional sociologists do, both within academia and outside of it. This chapter can help you see the writing you will do in its larger context—revealing sociology as an intellectual activity rather than just a body of knowledge.

Chapter 2 offers strategies for several different kinds of assignments you may encounter in sociology classes. While these may not be explicitly connected to the signature genre of sociology—the journal article based on original research—we believe that you can approach these classroom genres more productively if you think of them in relation to parts of the research enterprise.

Chapter 3 deals with a more extensive type of research paper, one that involves library sources beyond required class readings. We'll tell you how to set yourself up for success by thinking in terms of a question you are trying to answer with your library research, and by running your ideas past your professor in the form of a prospectus.

Chapters 4, 5, and 6 discuss the basic "moves" needed to write a complete research report describing your original research. We take you from the very beginning of the research process in Chapter 4—how to choose a fruitful research question—and describe how to connect the research question and the literature. Chapters 5 and 6 take you through the major components of the research report, including the abstract, introduction, methods, argument, literature review, and discussion of findings.

Chapters 7 and 8 help you understand how to use the work of others ethically and expertly in your own writing. There are tips on evaluating sources and guidance for using sources to develop your own arguments. We give concrete advice on how to acknowledge the contributions of others and how to avoid plagiarism.

Chapter 9, which focuses on style, is not a detailed grammar manual. (There are lots of those available already.) Instead, you will learn how to write with a sociological "voice." We discuss what can be taken for granted and what needs to be spelled out for the reader. We explain how to make your arguments more compelling and review some vocabulary and writing practices that students often misuse.

Chapter 10 provides advice on polishing your papers and getting them to your professors in the most professional manner.

A note to teachers: Students often have the mistaken idea that, as professionals, we get our writing "right" on our first attempt, and that we ask them to revise because they are not yet good enough writers. They are generally quite surprised to find out how much we revise our early drafts and how much we value candid feedback on our work from trusted colleagues. We encourage you to discuss your writing life with your students, helping them understand the importance of developing a writing process that allows adequate time to write—with plenty of revision and editing.

ABOUT THE AUTHORS

CARY MOSKOVITZ is Director of Writing in the Disciplines at Duke University. His articles and essays related to the teaching of writing have appeared in such publications as *The Chronicle of Higher Education*, *Science*, *College Composition and Communication*, and *Liberal Education*. He has served as a consultant on writing pedagogy and writing in the undergraduate curriculum for a number of US colleges and universities. His research interests include student writing in the undergraduate science curriculum, new approaches to providing feedback to student writing (including audio feedback techniques and the Duke Reader Project), and text recycling in scientific writing.

LYNN SMITH-LOVIN is Robert L. Wilson Professor of Arts and Sciences in the Department of Sociology (with secondary appointments in Psychology and Neuroscience and in Women's Studies) at Duke University. She received the 2006 Cooley-Mead Award for lifetime achievement in social psychology from the American Sociological Association Section on Social Psychology and the 2005 Lifetime Achievement Award from the ASA Section on Sociology of Emotions. She has served as the President of the Southern Sociological Society and as Vice President of the American Sociological Association. Her research examines the relationships among identity, action, and emotion, working within the affect control theory tradition, which examines how cultural information is imported into local social interactions and leads to behavioral, cognitive, and emotional responses.

ACKNOWLEDGMENTS

We would like to acknowledge the help of Linda Burton and Rebecca Bach, who participated in a Duke program to improve writing in the Sociology Department. We also received valuable input from Kieran Healy, Steve Vaisey, Chris Bail, Martin Ruef, Kenneth Spenner, Glibert Merx, Mark Chaves, Jim Moody, Eduardo Bonilla-Silva, and many other faculty members at Duke. Our students in FOCUS seminars, a senior research seminar, and a second-year graduate paper workshop provided useful feedback. Others who offered valuable comments from outside of Duke include Linda Francis, Dawn T. Robinson, Jody Clay-Warner, Justine Tinkler, Kathryn Lively, Kimberly Rogers, Christopher Moore, Perry Threlfall, Manashi Ray, our editors Tom Deans and Mya Poe, and our reviewers: Josh Ambrose, McDaniel College; Chris Anson, North Carolina State University; Michelle Bemiller, Walsh University; Wendy Cadge, Brandeis University; Shannon N. Davis, George Mason University; Lauri Dietz, DePaul University; Angela Green, University of Mississippi; Sarah K Harkness, The University of Iowa; David Kellogg, Coastal Carolina University; Eric Klinger, University of Colorado-Boulder; Kathryn Lively, Dartmouth College; Greggor Mattson, Oberlin College; Dan Melzer, California State University, Sacramento; Earl Mowatt, Bethune-Cookman University; Ethel Nicdao, University of the Pacific; Caroline Hodges Persell, New York University; Diane Pike, Augsburg College; Denise Rogers, University of Louisiana at Lafayette; Gene Theodori, Sam Houston State University; Lisa Slattery Walker, University of North Carolina Charlotte; Kassia Wosick, New Mexico State University; and Lorna Lueker Zukas, National University.

SOCIOLOGISTS AS WRITERS

Think of sociology as a big, ongoing conversation about human social life. In your first sociology classes, you may study the writings of some of those who first shaped the discipline—scholars like Durkheim and Weber. Reading such foundational work is like studying the transcripts of important past conversations.

If you focus your studies in sociology, you will also learn to read the "research literature." Entering the world of sociology research is like attending a large social event. People stand in clusters having different conversations (which correspond to articles and citations on different sociological questions). When you read the literature, you become an eavesdropper, listening in as current scholars discuss and debate their ideas and data—telling their colleagues about the questions they are asking, what they have learned, and what they still need to understand.

Because sociology covers so many social phenomena, there are hundreds of such conversations taking place simultaneously. Hang with one group for a while (i.e., read a number of articles in one research area) and you begin to understand a bit about that conversation.

Eventually the time will come for you to speak up, perhaps just restating something to see if you got it right (i.e., writing

FIGURE 1.1 Georg Simmel. Although he was one of the founders
of sociology, he was almost kicked out of graduate
school for sloppy writing on his dissertation.

about a text and perhaps venturing an evaluative comment). When you finally undertake a sociology research project of your own, you learn how to participate in the conversation. And if you publish your findings, your voice becomes part of the conversation.

For the field of sociology to develop, it needs new people to join the conversation, bringing their new ideas and perspectives. But joining the scholarly conversation requires *writing* sociology—and this isn't always easy. Even some of the founders of the discipline had their share of problems. Georg Simmel would go on to become one of the early influential sociologists, but his initial attempt at a PhD dissertation was rejected outright by his committee. Though it included an excellent ethnography and perhaps the first use of a questionnaire to collect sociological data (to study yodeling!), his examiners couldn't see past "the numerous misspellings and stylistic errors." One of his examiners, the great scientist Hermann von

FIGURE 1.2 W. E. B. DuBois. He argued unsuccessfully that
     "negro" should be capitalized.

Helmholtz, felt Simmel's writing was hopeless, remarking to
his colleagues, "We would be doing him a great service if we do
not encourage him further in this direction." Fortunately,
Simmel wasn't discouraged.

One of the earliest great American sociologists, W. E. B.
DuBois, had a rather different kind of writing problem—one
concerning ethical principles. In the early 1900s, the word
"negro" (the formal term used at that time for Blacks) wasn't
capitalized. Dubois felt strongly that it ought to be, and he
argued the point with his editor. Although he lost that battle,
sociologists eventually came around to his position—making
the capitalization of "Blacks" and "African Americans" standard practice.

Jane Addams, an early member of the "Chicago School" of
Sociology and the second woman to win the Nobel Peace
Prize, shows how varied inspiration for writing can be. She
first became interested in the poor while reading Charles

FIGURE 1.3 Jane Addams. Inspired by tales of human hardship in
the novels of Dickens and Tolstoy, she wrote about
the plight of the poor both in research papers and
memoirs.

Dickens's novels. From Tolstoy's book *My Religion*—which
argues that the rich should work with the poor—she got ideas
for new social programs she wanted to create. And she became
an accomplished writer herself. She composed influential research reports documenting the geography of typhoid fever
and showing that poor workers bore the brunt of illness. She
also wrote up her memoirs of Hull House, the settlement
house she founded to help poor neighborhoods. Like Dubois,
Addams felt a strong ethical sensibility about her writing—so
much so that she turned down a professorship at the University of Chicago because she didn't want any university to have
influence on her politically charged writing.

Some famous sociologists have cared so much about writing in the field that they have written about it. C. Wright Mills
wrote an essay about sociology writing titled "On Intellectual

Craftsmanship." Among other topics, he gives advice on organization and writing process—urging sociologists to write their ideas for a given project on notecards and then shuffle them around until they make sense. Robert K. Merton, one of the giants of the field, even wrote a parody that pokes fun at the tendency of some sociologists to use a lot of big words without saying much. The paper was facetiously titled "Foreword to a Preface for an Introduction to a Prolegomenon to a Discourse on a Certain Subject."

Sociology in Context

Many sociologists work at colleges or universities, and they write mostly about their own research. The audiences for their writing are mainly other academics who are trying to develop new knowledge in their area of specialty—and students, like you.

But most people who get degrees in sociology don't become professors. They often become lawyers, social workers, government officials, marketers, journalists, activists, or consultants. Their writing is different from that of academic sociologists. Those who work in industry write mainly for their employers—perhaps managers who want to use findings from sociological research to help them make good business decisions. Sociologists who work in government or nonprofit domains often write to inform the public about social patterns. Or they may try to influence policymakers by providing sociological insight about the possible impacts of new laws and regulations.

To better understand these differences, imagine how sociologists in three different settings might write about the US Tea Party political movement. A sociology professor might conduct a study to learn how segregation by educational level affects support for the Tea Party. She might find that people with more education support the Tea Party at higher rates than less educated people, and that the relationship is stronger when highly educated people are clumped in neighborhoods together . . . or she might find rather different trends. But regardless of what she concludes, this professor doesn't write about her research to influence the Tea Party movement. She writes to explore sociological ideas—in this case learning whether neighborhood homogeneity makes people's opinions stronger by limiting their exposure to different ideas and information.

A sociologist working for a marketing company might study how people respond to political ads the company had produced. This researcher might show two groups of people different descriptions of the Tea Party—one showing supporters happily waving flags and tea bags, and another of people describing what the government has done that makes them angry. The company will use this research to learn how viewers respond to the ads, with the goal of increasing political donations.

Our third sociologist works for a nonpartisan, nonprofit political research organization. He is hired to study trends in Tea Party support among different demographic groups—people of different ages, races, and education levels. His employer uses that information to speculate on how the Tea Party movement might affect the next election. The goal of the organization is to gather useful information to be disseminated to the public. They want to inform the debate, not change a particular outcome.

Now that you have a sense for why sociologists write in different contexts, let's look at *what* they write.

Sociological Writing in Academia

Sociology professors write in a variety of genres. They write *literature reviews*—summarizing and synthesizing published research done by others and offering directions for new research. They might write in-depth analyses of a single book or article someone else has written in the form of a *book review* or *comment*. And although academic sociologists usually write for other academics, they sometimes address a broader public audience—perhaps in a blog or a newspaper *op-ed column* advocating a policy position. Mostly though, sociology professors write about their own research in the form of *research reports*. These reports may be journal articles, book chapters, or even entire books. Because doing research costs money, professors also regularly write *research proposals* to funding agencies to raise the funds to carry out new research.

Sociologists study a wide variety of phenomena, from interactions between individuals (parents and their children, workers and bosses, and so on) to interactions between entire nations. Their methods are diverse, too, ranging from mathematical modeling and statistical analysis (similar to what natural scientists do) to on-the-ground observation of people doing whatever they naturally do (more like what cultural anthropologists do). Because of this variety, the structure of sociology research reports varies tremendously. Yet despite this variety, sociologists have similar goals for their research: to contribute to a cumulative body of knowledge about some aspect of social life.

Regardless of topic or method, the sociologist's research is driven by questions: Why did something happen? How did it happen? What are the crucial differences between two situations? Why do two groups of people experience different outcomes? These questions are parts of the big sociological puzzle.

But such questions and answers don't matter to the world of sociology until the author *writes* about the research. Sociologists must describe their research clearly and make a compelling argument about how their work helps to answer their research question. Sociologists' attempts to answer these questions are connected to one another through what we call a "literature"—a body of research reports written about similar questions. Authors decide which question to work on next by studying the literature. They look for gaps among the questions that have already been asked and answered, and then figure out how to gather evidence that might help answer new questions.

For example, Elizabeth McClintock (2014) was intrigued by published research suggesting that as men and women form couples, women "exchange" their beauty for men's status. But McClintock thought that these researchers were ignoring another sociological perspective—that people tend to seek out others *like* themselves. And she wondered whether the reverse situation might also be true: Might *men* sometimes "trade" looks for status with women? Through her research, she found that people *do* tend to choose partners of similar physical attractiveness and status—and once she controlled for that tendency, it appeared that women and men were equally likely to trade looks for status.

McClintock's research was important because it corrected an important misunderstanding in the sociological literature. But she couldn't just say, "Hey folks, turns out I'm right and you're wrong." She had to write—explaining in careful detail how she did her research, so skeptical readers could evaluate *for themselves* whether to accept her conclusions. Her research then became part—an important part—of that literature.

Collecting high-quality data on humans is more complicated than collecting data in a chemistry lab. So, like many sociologists, McClintock didn't collect her own data but used a "database"—a large data set compiled by others to facilitate sociological inquiry. For her research, McClintock used the National Longitudinal Study of Adolescent Health (Add Health) Romantic Pair Sample—a sample of about 1,500 dating, cohabiting, and married couples in the United States.

These large, publicly available (even to you!) data sets are like a public library—but for data rather than books. There are so many variables in these data sets that researchers could ask an almost infinite number of interesting questions of them. And using such high-quality, publicly available data gives readers a lot of confidence in the research—and therefore more confidence in findings based on them. (You'll find more about these publically available data sources in Chapter 4, especially the "Developing a Research Question" section.)

While research reports contribute new evidence to the field, *literature reviews* offer syntheses of existing studies—analyzing the published work of other researchers who have studied a common topic. Good examples of reviews can be found in the *Annual Review of Sociology*—one of the most highly regarded publications in the field.

In the most cited review ever published in this journal, Alejandro Portes examined research on "social capital"—the connections to other people that can be used to achieve good outcomes. Even though Portes didn't report new research of his own, the article made an important intellectual contribution: Some researchers had been trying to apply the concept of social capital to organizations, communities, and even entire societies, which Portes argued was not valid. Others have disagreed, yet almost every scholar who defines social capital as a characteristic of *people* (rather than some larger social unit) cites Portes's review to support their definition. And even researchers who apply the social capital concept to communities are likely *still* to cite Portes's review to make a clear distinction between individual and community social capital.

Reviews can be articles or full-length books. They can focus on a concept (like Portes's paper on social capital), a theory, a process, a special group of people, and so on. The essential thing about a review is that it creates a framework for viewing the accumulated knowledge on a topic. The library research paper that we discuss in Chapter 3 is a student-level version of this task.

To be taken seriously as part of the scholarly literature, research reports and books must be "peer reviewed." In the peer-review process, the editor sends the submitted manuscript to a set of experts in the research area. These reviewers judge its contribution to the literature and its quality— and then make a recommendation to the editor about whether or not to publish it. The editor then makes the decision: publish, request a revision, or reject the article. We don't cover writing reviews in this book, but you should understand that the peer-review process is an important quality-control mechanism. When you read scholarly journals or books from academic presses, you know that several professional social scientists looked at the piece and thought it was good enough to publish.

In contrast to research reports, which present new research, and literature reviews, which summarize existing research, *research proposals* address work yet to be done. The audiences for these proposals are organizations offering grants to fund research. Proposals are similar to research reports, but without analyses or conclusions. They pose a question about social life, argue why it's important in terms of a sociological literature, and describe methods for collecting evidence. Grants are usually competitive, judged on their scientific merit by a panel of other scholars to determine which get funded. Proposals often have even more detail about methods of data collection than research reports, because they are trying to convince reviewers that the project can collect evidence in a way that will answer the question convincingly.

In addition to the research-related genres we've just described, academic sociologists sometimes communicate their thoughts on how sociological evidence relates to current debates through editorials or other opinion pieces—based on their analysis sociological research. Our colleague Angel

Harris wrote several such columns for *The New York Times* and other media outlets after he and coauthor Keith Robinson published *Broken Compass: Parental Involvement in Children's Education*. In this book, a highly technical discussion about multivariate analyses of survey data, Harris and Robinson argue that parenting behaviors such as helping with homework and attending school functions have little impact on the educational success of children. Thus, they conclude that government programs aimed at engaging parents in school aren't likely to have much impact. Professor Harris knew that his findings would be of interest to many people who wouldn't read such a technical book. Writing op-eds gave him a way to make his research accessible to the general public.

A growing number of academic sociologists are communicating their ideas to the broader public through blogs. Our colleague Kieran Healy used his blog (http://kieranhealy.org/blog/) to address social issues related to income inequality. He wrote about a fictional Gini Airline that allocated airplane seat space according to passenger income using the same proportions as the Gini coefficient—a measure of income inequality in the US population. On Gini, coach passengers are squeezed together even tighter than on real airlines today, whereas the richest four passengers get to share almost half of the entire cabin.

Sociological Writing in Workplaces Outside Academia

Sociologists who work outside of academia are often tasked with interpreting research for nonspecialists—whether the general public, their bosses, or clients. The motivations for such writing are quite diverse. Government agencies, think tanks, and other entities often commission sociologists to find sound, science-based solutions to public problems. These sociologists might write *position papers* that summarize current knowledge on a topic and offer research-based recommendations for policy. If the research needed to find a solution hasn't yet been done, the sociologist might suggest new research that the organization (or others) should sponsor.

Other types of organizations are not interested in sociology as a way to understand social behavior. Instead, they hire sociologists to construct arguments for positions they already hold or to refute policy proposals they see as undesirable. Using sociology research in this way isn't really doing science because the studies are "cherry picked" to support already-decided positions. But it does require sociological skill: locating and interpreting relevant research reports and communicating those findings in a convincing way.

There are also organizations that hire sociologists to conduct new research with the direct intent of informing the general public. The Pew Research Center, one of the most highly respected of such organizations, describes itself as "a nonpartisan fact tank that informs the public about the issues, attitudes, and trends shaping America and the world." To accomplish this aim, Pew conducts public opinion polls. One of their recent studies is titled: "As Global Threats Loom, More Say U.S. Does Too Little." This survey found that the share of Americans saying the United States doesn't do enough to address global problems nearly doubled between November 2013 and August 2014. Those who took the survey identified the Islamic militants known as ISIS or ISIL as the top US security threats.

Sociologists who work for Pew write easy-to-read reports for journalists and the public that describe the results of their polls—trying to be as descriptive and nonjudgmental as possible. The main differences between this type of writing and academic research are that its aims are short term and simply informative. There is no larger scientific literature in which the

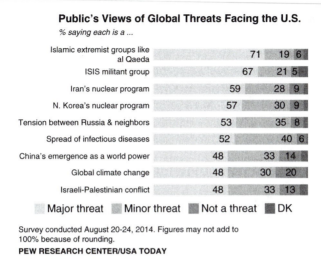

FIGURE 1.4 Example of sociology writing intended to inform the public.

research question is embedded. The questions are simply "What do people think about X right now?" Questions about *how* or *why* certain types of people think the way they do usually fall outside the scope of such reports.

While some nonacademic sociological writing is aimed at broad audiences such as the public or policymakers, other sociologists write for intentionally limited audiences—decision makers in business or marketing firms. These sociologists might do experiments or conduct focus group interviews to see how people respond to advertisements. Although their methods may be similar to those used in an academic study, such as random assignment to different conditions in an experiment, the purpose of their research and the writing they do is very different: to increase sales.

Intel, for example, employs over 100 social scientists to study how people think about and use computing technology.

They conduct focus groups, interview consumers, and sometimes invent innovative ways of finding out how people use products. One group of Intel researchers asked people to empty out their cars, photographing all of the objects removed. They then asked the car owners how and when they used that stuff (much of which contained Intel chips). Memos from studies like this have a function similar to position papers, but the goal is to help company managers make decisions.

SUCCEEDING AT COMMON SOCIOLOGY WRITING ASSIGNMENTS

In advanced sociology courses, assignments are often designed to introduce students to the practice of sociological research. In other courses, assignments aim to help students *learn* sociological concepts or *make connections* between their experiences and sociological ideas. If you are taking sociology classes as an undergraduate, you'll likely be assigned some of the latter, and this chapter offers strategies for handling them. Although we can't cover all of the possibilities, we have picked some common writing tasks.

Even if your assignment doesn't look quite like any of those we've included, you'll likely find that many of the principles we discuss in this chapter apply. And ideas from later chapters dealing with sociological research will be relevant, too. Although the assignments we discuss in this chapter don't involve doing actual sociological research, many of their underlying objectives and features correspond to *parts* of research-oriented writing tasks. So when ideas from other chapters apply here, we'll point them out.

Although the assignments we discuss in this chapter are rather different from one another, they have similar goals: to help you understand the sociological concepts and processes you've been studying and apply them in a new context. This is true even for the assignments that ask you to write about your own experiences. Let's say, for example, that you're required to keep a journal of experiences illustrating sociological ideas from class. You might think your teacher expects you to write something like a diary, but he'll probably want something more analytical. You'll need to use your personal experiences in the same way that an academic sociologist would use ethnographic observations to reveal a social process or concept. The assignment is based on your experience, but it isn't really *about* you.

Want to Do More Than Just Meet Expectations?

Professors love it when students apply ideas from other classes they have taken. If you think of a concept or process you learned about in another sociology class (or even a different social science class) that applies to your case, discuss that, too! Just make sure it's relevant.

Book or Article Review

If you are assigned to review an article or book, your instructor will likely constrain your choice of readings—perhaps by providing a list of texts from which you can pick. The assignment may tell you to "evaluate" or "analyze" the text, but that doesn't necessarily mean your professor expects you to identify an important flaw in this published work of scholarship (although it *is* sometimes possible).

Your first step, obviously, is to read the text (and you may need to read it more than once). Keep in mind that your review should both summarize the main ideas and offer your own insight about the text. So as you read, take notes. (If you are reviewing something short enough, consider printing a copy and making notes on the pages; but even if using a PDF or Word document, you can insert comments as you go.) Note things that seem essential to the aim of the text—central questions or theses, key definitions, conclusions, and so on.

Look for indicators of the authors' intentions early on— perhaps in the Introduction or Foreword. What is the main question the authors are addressing? What do the authors say is new about what they are doing? Are they challenging established ideas? How does this text contribute to the scientific literature? If you are reviewing a research report, look at our discussion in Chapter 5 about the typical "moves" in a research introduction. Identifying these moves in your assigned text will help you locate places where the authors explain their work in these terms.

Most likely, the objective of your review assignment is to help you learn sociological ideas rather than produce a professional-style review. If that's the case, it's fine to focus your review on what *you* got out of the text. So make notes on what strikes your interest: What new ideas are you learning? What do you find surprising? How does what you are reading relate to sociological concepts you have studied in class? Does the text offer similar ideas or a contrasting view? And so on. These notes are your dialogue with the text.

Be sure to read the text all the way through, paying close attention to figures and tables. When it's time to start drafting, begin your review by introducing the work:

- What are the main questions it is addressing?
- How do the authors attempt to answer that question (e.g., with what type of evidence)?
- What sociological concepts do they use to frame their work?

Next, summarize the argument, evidence, and conclusions of the text in some detail. Imagine you were having coffee with your professor and that she has not read that book or article.

How would you explain what the authors were up to, what methods they used, and what conclusions they reached?

Remember that your professors are looking for you to tie the specifics of this text to broader sociological concepts from the class. You might explain how the book or article has helped to fill a knowledge gap in the research literature. You might describe how this piece contributes to your knowledge about some course topic or provides a good example of a process that you've discussed in class. For example, if you've been learning about the sociology of emotions and almost all of the class readings are on gender differences, you could point out that Adia Wingfield's (2010) paper on emotion work among Black professional men was useful in bringing race into the field. *This* is the type of evaluation and analysis that your professor wants.

Your Role as a "Critic"

Your professor doesn't really care whether you like the article or book, or if you found it interesting. She surely doesn't want to know if you think that it should have been written about some other, more interesting (to you) topic. The point of the assignment is to show that you are a competent reader of sociological literature, and that you can relate this new piece of knowledge to the mosaic of sociological concepts that your professor has been putting together through the class readings. You can best accomplish this task by moving back and forth between your description of specific aspects of the reading and discussions of more abstract concepts from the class.

If you are reviewing a book rather than an article, you might look to see if others have reviewed it. For major books there might be three or four reviews; these are typically written within a couple of years of the publication date. It's not cheating to refer to other people's ideas in your review, so long as you do so judiciously. Do not use their ideas as a substitute for your own review and be sure to cite them generously. Be especially careful not to use other reviews to construct a patchwork essay (see pp. 192–194). Should you find a phrase or sentence in a review that seems especially interesting or pithy, you may decide to quote it. But remember that whether you quote, paraphrase, or summarize: if you use ideas from another review, you need to cite it. That means you'll need a reference section even for this short paper, giving the full citation for this and any other sources you use.

Before turning in your paper, don't forget about a title. It might begin with "A review of [the name of the book or article you are reviewing]," followed by a subtitle that names some major conceptual or theoretical point that seemed salient in your analysis.

Models of Book Reviews

Contemporary Sociology is the American Sociological Association's book review journal and publishes hundreds of reviews every year. Skim a few examples for ideas about how to begin and end, for tone, and for overall structure. The *American Journal of Sociology* and *Social Forces* also publish a book review section in each issue. Most major sociology books will have been reviewed in all three of these outlets.

Case Study

The case study is a widely used type of educational writing, so here, too, you can find good, professionally written examples. The Harvard Business School is famous for using cases. As with the book review assignment, the main goal of a case study is to use the context of some organization or other entity to illustrate or examine sociological concepts. Whereas the book review focuses on a text, the case study focuses on an organization or group (or even a country at some point in history) and invites you to bring general sociological principles to bear on it.

Describing the Case

Questions can help you tell the story.

Who? Who are the actors? How are they connected?

Where? Where do they interact, and what are the relevant features of those environments? Were they a part of some larger organization or institution? What was its structure and purpose?

What and why? What were the actors trying to do? How did the doers perceive their circumstances? What did they do to achieve their goals? What resources did they have and use?

What happened? What problems or challenges were encountered? What were the intended and unintended consequences of the actions taken? How did others view these results, and how did they respond?

How do the events illustrate sociological processes and concepts?

A major component of the case study is describing the organization and its context. Because case studies involve complex settings with multiple players, writing this description requires considerable thought. You need to give readers a clear understanding of who did what and why. Your description of the case should establish the setting, introduce the characters and their motivations and concerns, and then lay out the narrative. Think of this part as telling the story of the case.

After you have thoroughly described the case, explain how it illustrates important social processes—especially the processes that have been emphasized in your class. Remember that the purpose of the case is to illustrate concepts. Be explicit about the connections between concepts and this story by relating specific details from the case to the concepts, and vice versa. Try to work back and forth between writing about the events and the concepts that they are supposed to illustrate. If in your first draft you end up with a descriptive section and a separate sociological section, that's a problem; revise your paper, interweaving the two parts into a more seamless discussion.

You may find it difficult to write about such connections with your professor in mind because you'll think these connections are obvious to her. If so, try to write for a different audience—someone who knows the basics of sociology but who does not know the specific concepts you are studying in this class.

Models of Case Studies

Many case studies are published, which means you can find good examples of what you are trying to do. Although your assignment may be shorter than typical published examples, they can still help you get a feel for the genre. The Harvard Case Studies are particularly good, but there are many others. Your librarian can help you locate some.

Experience Essay

Sociology teachers often ask students to illustrate a concept discussed in class by describing a personal experience. Your professor might want you to write an essay or memoir, reflecting on how experiences in your own life illustrate sociological processes. Or perhaps you'll be asked to keep a journal, write a blog post, or use some other form of social media to share your experiences and analyses.

For any of these types of assignments, the key is to frame your experiences as *examples* of abstract concepts rather than just as vivid accounts of things that happened to you. In other words, write about your social experiences or observations as the demonstration of a sociological principle relevant to the course. As much as your professor cares about his students, he didn't assign this task to get to know you better as a person. He is interested in how well you can apply and communicate your understanding of sociology.

Your life is filled with experiences that are sociologically interesting, so you have lots of examples from which to choose. These kinds of assignments will be easier if you begin by intentionally selecting an experience that reflects the focus of your class. In a class on gender, you might think of a specific interaction between men and women. In a more general sociology class, you might write about experiences involving members of different organizations, or different places on campus (classrooms, dining halls, gyms), or groups of students on different career paths or majors.

Using "I" is Okay!

We discuss this issue even more in Chapter 9 on Style (see pp. 201–206), but the Experience Essay is a clear case. You are writing about your own experiences, so feel free to use "I" all you want.

An easy but effective way to begin writing is by crafting a title for your essay, journal entry, or blog. A title can keep your attention on what matters most—the link between the experience and the concepts. Try a two-part title: a very short description of the specific event followed by the name of the concept or process you are illustrating. "Interruptions in a Lunchtime Conversation: Gender and Status as Control of the Topic" would be fitting if you discuss how patterns of talk between you and your friends illustrate how males and females get different levels of "floor time" in casual conversations and what that says about typical status differences between men and women.

Once you have a title, try one of the following structures for making the needed connections between experience and concepts. One begins with the experience, the other with the concept.

Option 1: Begin by describing your experience vividly, focusing on the few details that either illustrate the sociological idea or challenge it. Then refer back to those details, one at a time, explaining how they relate to particular aspects of the sociology.

Option 2: Begin similarly to the introduction of a research report. (See Introductions, moves 1 and 2, pp. 88–91.) Start by naming and summarizing the sociological topic and then giving a brief overview of some relevant sociological literature to present the relevant theory. (For a short assignment, this literature might be selected from readings for your class.) After that mini-intro, describe your experience as evidence, illustration, or example—beginning with a description of the specific scene or context and moving to a detailed account of the experience—remembering to tie the key details to the theory or concept as for option 1.

Quotations can be useful when discussing theory, but keep them brief—especially if they are from class readings (because you know your teacher is familiar with that material). If a short phrase from a source captures the core of the concept, weave it into a sentence of your own. Even if you use a quotation, be sure to describe the concept or process in your own words, too.

Writing the Experience Essay

Explain your experiences as examples of sociology concepts from the class rather than just vivid accounts of things that happened to you.

Two good options for structure:

- First describe the experience, emphasizing details that relate to the sociological concept. Then, explain how the details relate to the concept.
- Start by describing the theory or concept. Then, describe the experience—connecting the details to the sociology as you go.

Want to Do More Than Just Meet Expectations?

- Include a *contrasting* experience—even a hypothetical one if it's realistic.
- Avoid simplistic comparisons. Rather than pretending your experience maps perfectly onto the theory, acknowledge and discuss aspects of your experience that *do not* seem to fit. Even better—relate those details to a competing theory or a different concept if you know of one.

Student experience essays often suffer from insufficient framing or focus. While most students write about both their own experience and the sociology, many fail to build the paper around the *connections* between them. Once you have written a draft, look at it carefully. Do you see two distinct parts—one that discusses only the sociology and another that describes only your experience? If so, you haven't done enough to link the two. There should be a considerable amount of connecting material—explanation, analysis—that doesn't fit cleanly into one of those two categories, material that shuttles between the sociological principles and your own observations, often in the same sentence.

To help you make those connections explicit, imagine the audience as someone who wanted you to teach them the sociology concepts, rather than your professor or graduate teaching assistant. As a student writer, it feels odd to explain something to your teacher, who first explained it to you! Yet this is probably what your professor wants you to do. Imagine again that your topic was gender and status as it relates to conversation. You would need to explain why interruptions might be interpreted as controlling the topic of conversation. Then, you might describe how gender could be considered a status characteristic, with men being accorded greater respect than women—generally as well as in conversation. Only then would an experience where men had dominated a lunchtime conversation by interrupting women and changing the topic *become* an illustration of status and gender.

If you want to write an exceptional experience essay, move beyond simply discussing an experience that demonstrates a concept by also including a *contrasting* experience. Our gender/talk example would be made even stronger by contrasting it with a conversation in a domain in which women are generally regarded to have higher status—like fashion, color, or childrearing. If women interrupted and dominated the conversation more than men in this context, the example would be even clearer, because of the comparison between the two domains.

Your Life Is Filled With "Data"

You might think about the descriptions of your experiences or observations as qualitative data in an informal research report. In Chapter 6 (pp. 121–128) we discuss how to write the Results section of original qualitative research. That can be a guide for describing your experiences.

Internship Report

Colleges are increasingly looking for ways to help students maximize the educational value of their internship experiences. Sociology programs may do this by asking students to write formal reflections on their internships through the lens of sociological theory. This "internship report" is essentially a hybrid of the case study and the experience essay—it's a case study in which you are imbedded as a participant-observer.

A good way to begin is with a description of the organization where you interned—like in the "Describing the Case" box on p. 20. The goal of the organization will almost always be an important point of this description. Also describe the role you took during your internship. Be careful not to fill up this introduction with random details. Decide which parts of the organization's environment were important during the period of your internship—your "case." Focus your description on those elements that relate to sociological theories and key concepts you've studied. For example, if you've learned that size, demographic composition, and status structure are important to organizations, include details about those things. What social processes were you embedded in that made a difference to what you were able to accomplish? Or just as important, and perhaps more interesting—what made it difficult to get things done?

Writing the Internship Report: Take Notes Along the Way

Although your experience may seem unforgettable while you're in it, it will be hard to recall the details important for writing your report after it's over. Before you begin the internship make a list of things you would need to know to write a good case study of the organization. During the internship you can fill in those details. Just a few minutes of note-taking each day will give you plenty of material to work with. Making notes along the way also allows you to ask questions at the right moments. (Asking smart questions is also a great way to make a good impression.) When someone says something particularly memorable, try to jot down her exact words. Having a few short quotes will give your report a vividness that it would otherwise lack. Because the goal of the report is to improve your understanding of sociology concepts, you'll do well to read some sociology theory during your internship—thinking about your organization as you do.

For the core of your internship report, the key is to generalize from your particular experience. As with the case study, avoid the temptation to first tell the entire story of your summer or semester and write about sociological theory afterward. Once you have laid out your setting, move frequently back and forth between things that happened and relevant concepts.

Writing this part of your internship report has quite a bit in common with using ethnographic or in-depth interview data in an original research paper. Turn to Chapter 6 and read the description of how to use qualitative observations in a Results section (pp. 121–128). Many of the same principles apply here. You might find that e-mail exchanges are good sources of qualitative data; but if you choose to quote from these in your report, be sure to get written permission from whoever wrote them.

You can end your report by summarizing the major concepts illustrated by your "case" and posing questions about sociology that your experience raised. Given your experience, what would you like to learn more about? Did any aspect of your experience challenge some standard sociological concepts?

Internship Research Projects

Organizations sometimes ask interns to do a research project as part of their work. An intern working for a university's Department of Recreation might design a satisfaction survey for the school's intramural programs. At a local arts council, an intern might interview participants in an arts program to see how they learned about the program to help improve their marketing strategies.

An internship report for such a research experience might begin like the case-study model described earlier. You'd describe the organization, its goals, and your place within it. But then your report should shift to something more like a research report (see Chapters 5 and 6, sections on Methods and Results). You'll have a research question, which you should state clearly and explicitly. For example, the university physical education intern might research the question, "What factors impact the experience of participating in the university's sports clubs and how satisfied are current members with their experience?" That's a good question. Note that unlike the research questions described in Chapter 4, your internship research question will be dictated by your organization. And because it's applied rather than scholarly research, it won't be framed as making a contribution to a scientific literature.

Although your project will likely be directed to help further some organizational goal, don't overstate your contribution to the organization. When explaining the goals of your project, be clear about what you actually set out to *do* in your research, given the available time and resources. The arts council intern, for example, might be tempted to say that her project was to "evaluate the effectiveness of the organization's marketing strategies." However, because she only surveyed program participants, she really addressed more limited issues: "How do our participants learn about the activities that they attend? Do they participate in social media? Would they like to hear more about our activities through those channels?" Professors will not be disappointed in your acknowledging such limitations; rather, they'll welcome that you have a good understanding of what you did (and didn't) do. On the other hand, don't be shy in stressing the contributions that you *do* make. Remember that this assignment is designed for you to showcase your work—it's one place where showing off a bit is totally appropriate.

Following your explanation of the research task, you'll need to describe your methods. Do this at a level of detail that will keep your reader's interest and focus—including what they need to know but not irrelevant detail. Lengthy material such as your actual questionnaire and description of variables can be put in an appendix; this will improve the flow of your text. Finally, present your results and the conclusions that you drew from those findings as they are relevant to your organization. Before you leave, or soon after your return, try to get feedback on your document from people in the organization.

Although this is a type of research report, it's more like a workplace report than an academic one. Some of the guidance we give about writing scholarly research reports applies here— but some doesn't. Our general guidance on writing Methods and Results sections applies here: Walk your reader through your results one step at a time; point clearly to the features of tables and figures you want them to notice; and be consistent in your language when referring to variables or concepts. On the other hand, your introduction, background, and conclusion sections will be rather different; instead of framing these parts in relation to the scholarly literature, you'll want to discuss them in relation to the organization and its goals.

Regardless of the type of internship you do, keep the report clearly connected to sociology theory. Imagine your favorite sociology professor reading your report. You want her to think: "Wow—this student was really able to take ideas we studied in class and apply them in context." The whole point of an internship is to connect your sociological learning with a work setting.

Response to Literature, Film, or Other Cultural Products

The experience essay discussed earlier asks you to look at an event from your own life through a sociological lens. Your professor might assign a similar kind of writing—but one based on a work of fiction, film, visual art, product presentation, or other artifact. Because the goals of these assignments are similar, most of our advice for writing the experience essay applies here as well.

The trick here is to figure out which specific features of the object of study you should focus on in your paper. Think about your course: What concepts and processes have you been discussing in class? Those are the things you'll want to discuss in your response essay. You might begin by giving some background on the sociological phenomenon that you'll be discussing. If you are writing about a story in which a US family struggles financially with a medical emergency, you might start by explaining that the United States comprises only

5 percent of the world's population, but it is responsible for half of the world's expenditures on health care. Then you could go on to explain how inequality shapes access to care in the United States and move on to the specific types of inequality featured in the story. As we explained for the experience essay, try to move beyond the one-idea/one-example form by looking for contrasting examples. You might contrast the family described earlier with another in the story (or in another story) that has different characteristics (e.g., different levels of education, employment characteristics, or family structures in another country). Don't be afraid to bring in ideas or examples from other works, too—as long as they enrich your analysis of the assigned object of study rather than taking attention away from it.

Let's look at one more example. If you were analyzing an advertisement for women's beauty products, you might begin with a reference to an academic source about gendered appeals (perhaps Goffman's *Gender Advertisements*)—summarizing the main ideas. Then you'd describe specific features of the ad that illustrate those ideas. Again, contrast often works: You might look at some ads for men's products to see how they are similar (e.g., young, sexy, scantily clothed) and how they are different (e.g., direct gaze rather than averted gaze, dominant rather than submissive poses).

It's important to approach any of these assignments as serious academic work requiring time for reflection and revision. You might think that because you are being asked to respond to a piece of fiction, art, or popular culture rather than an academic text, your first reactions are sufficient. Such off-the-cuff responses might be fine for a Yelp review, but they won't impress your professor. Take the time to craft a fine essay. Make sure every paragraph develops some point relevant to the case you are making and work out a meaningful structure for the essay.

Things to Remember in Responding to Fiction or Art

- It's not about you: your professor doesn't want to know whether or not you liked the film or how you felt about the protagonist of a vignette. The art is only a vehicle for discussing the sociology.
- Choose the descriptive detail you want to include carefully. Don't repeat the entire vignette or narrative for your professor. Only mention the features that you are going to tie to the course material. This is especially true if the professor *gave* you the story to analyze; if you chose your own story, film, or advertisement, you might need to provide more description so your professor can understand it.
- Use professional language, statements of research findings, and citations to all sources—not merely your unsupported opinions. You aren't telling a buddy about this film; you are presenting a perspective to your professor.
- Move from the specifics of the narrative to the abstract concepts, processes, and patterns—but avoid meaningless overgeneralizations such as "everyone knows," "it's impossible not to," or "it is always . . ."
- If you are an international student, you might point out parts of the fiction or artwork that contain implicit cultural content that mean different things to you, as someone from another culture.

STRATEGIES FOR WRITING THE LIBRARY RESEARCH PAPER

Sociology professors often assign something they call a "research paper," and unfortunately, they can use this same term to refer to two rather different types of projects. They might use the term as a synonym for what we will call the *research report*—reports of original research as published in *journal articles*. That's the main type of writing most of your professors do in their own work. If you are an undergraduate majoring in sociology, you might be asked to do something like this as a capstone experience toward the end of your studies. If you are a graduate student, this type of writing will be a focus of your training. The other meaning is what we are going to call the *library research paper*. It's *research* because you are expected to use sources other than the texts assigned for the class; you *research* a topic or question.

Because this is a common point of confusion, we want to be clear: For the *library research* paper, which we discuss in this chapter, you are expected to locate, summarize, synthesize, and analyze what *others* have written on a topic. For the *research report*, which we discuss in in Chapters 4, 5, and 6, you collect and analyze original data of your own. Even though the library research paper and the research report are different kinds of writing, they have some overlapping features. In particular, library research papers are similar to literature reviews that are an essential component of research reports.

Keep in mind an important difference, too: Although professors' expectations for research reports are based largely on professional conventions, professors tend to have individualized expectations for library research papers. And if that didn't offer enough potential confusion, the research papers you are assigned in sociology will likely be different from what your professors in *other* departments call "research papers."

So pay close attention to the specifications for each assignment. Some professors may encourage you to use a mix of different kinds of sources; others may require peer-reviewed sources exclusively. In one class, the paper might be a relatively small assignment. In another, it could be the major determinant of your grade. But despite the differences, the essential tasks for most of these assignments are similar: locate relevant sources, synthesize them (comparing and contrasting their ideas or findings), engage in critical sociological thinking, and draw reasonable conclusions based on what you found.

Start Smart: A Question and a Prospectus

Many students approach library research papers as investigations of a topic. But *topics* do not give sufficient focus to research. We suggest that before beginning your research, you move from a topic to a *question*. A question will give you a tighter and more interesting research agenda.

The assignment prompt may ask you to "develop a thesis" or "make an argument" or "demonstrate your sociological imagination." Such phrases mean that your instructor expects a paper that's more than a sequence of summaries of your sources. Starting out with an interesting question will help you make meaningful connections among the sources that you choose.

Because instructors' requirements for library research papers vary so much, you'll do yourself a big favor by making sure you are on the right track before getting too far from the station. A great way to do this is to begin by drafting a "prospectus"—a brief statement explaining what you are planning to do and how you plan to do it.

Relevant Advice for Developing a Research Question

For detailed advice on choosing a good research question, see Developing a Research Question in Chapter 4 (pp. 56–73). Although you won't be gathering new evidence for your library research paper, you can use the specific strategies and examples in that section to ensure that your question has a sociological focus. Here are some of the main points.

1. *Make your question sociological.* Be sure it's connected to some existing sociological research and abstract enough to apply to an array of social situations.
2. *Make your question narrow enough.* Students almost always start with questions that are much too broad—questions that would require an entire book or maybe a career's worth of research to answer in a meaningful way. Once you have an idea for a question, narrow it down more and more until it's about as narrow as it can be without violating #1.
3. *Find a core research article that interests you.* Use that article as a springboard for a related question: This author studied X; but what about Y? This author asked Z, but did other people who addressed that question find the same results? If this author suggested future research on the topic, did others follow up? What did they find?

Write this prospectus soon after getting the assignment and set up a meeting with your professor to discuss it before proceeding. This may be the single most useful thing you can do to develop an excellent paper. Here's why:

- It is not uncommon for students to misunderstand something about library research assignments. They might, for example, choose an inappropriate question or use the wrong kinds of sources. Getting feedback from your instructor on a prospectus gets you headed in a promising direction before you invest too much time heading down the wrong path.
- It can help you avoid writer's block and procrastination.
- It provides focus for your library research and reading.
- It's a great document to take to a librarian to get help finding just the right sources. (Bring the assignment details, too!)

If your professor suggests that you do some things differently than you had planned, see that as a major success. It means you saved yourself either the time and effort of going in the wrong direction or the disappointing grade you would have received had you not corrected course.

If you aren't sure what to include in your prospectus, here's an outline. Start with the headings (underlined in the following list), adding to each section as you get ideas and find materials.

- *A **working title** in the form of a question*—the question you are focusing on.
- *A paragraph explaining **why the question is sociologically interesting**.* Does your question relate to a current or ongoing social or policy problem? Does a specific case or situation you are interested in challenge an accepted theory?

- *A paragraph stating your initial **hypothesis** about what you expect the answer of your question to be, and why.* We know it seems odd to state a hypothesis before you've done any research. But as long as you consider this hypothesis provisional, it can provide focus to your research. Instead of merely looking for sources on a topic, you can look for material that supports or challenges your hypothesis. Because you chose your hypothesis before knowing much about the question, you should be just as likely to change your position as to keep it!
- *A list of possible **references**.* Even better, make two lists: "background references" that present the theory and information needed to understand your question, and "evidence references" that can help you answer the question. Have at least two or three items in each category before talking with your instructor so you can make sure it's the right kind of source.

Doing the Library Research

Once you have a reasonably focused question, it's time to start the library research for real. To write a good paper, you need to approach the process of selecting your sources as a serious activity that will take time and thought, rather than as something you do before you get down to the real work.

Your library research assignments may specify a target or minimum number of references to use. (If it doesn't, ask your professor to suggest a reasonable range.) Let's say you are supposed to find 10–15 references for your paper. You *could* just use the first 10 or so you find that have any relevance to your project, but if you want to write a good paper, you're setting a trap for yourself. Writing a successful research paper requires making *meaningful* connections among your sources and drawing interesting conclusions. If you don't select your articles and books strategically, you'll have a hard time bringing them together in a coherent way.

Google Scholar or other search engines can be a reasonable place to start. These search tools can give you a sense of whether there is too little or way too much published research relevant to your question—which can help you know if you need to narrow or broaden the scope of your project. Looking at some of the good hits can help you identify some key terms to use as you continue your searches. But these open-access search tools don't give you access to all of the published research. Publishers require payment for access to most of their materials—and this is what much of your school's library budget is used for. To have access to the full range of possible sources, you'll need to go through your school's library website and work from one of their "library databases."

Tips for Finding a Literature

We discuss how to use library databases effectively in Chapter 4: Finding a Literature (pp. 74–80). The research task you are doing is very similar to what we describe there, just not as extensive.

- Locate one article closely related to that you your research question. Use it to find other sources by (1) checking its reference list and (2) seeing what sources cited this one. (You can do this with some databases, including Web of Science and Scopus.)
- Seek out a librarian to help you master library databases as soon as you have a rough idea of what you want to do—perhaps after you have the first couple of paragraphs of your prospectus written. The librarian

can help you fill out the last part of the prospectus: the sample references.

- Try searching with different keywords and phrases. Look at any relevant articles that you *do* find to learn the terms they use to describe the subjects.
- If you are getting many hits that aren't related to your research question, use the "not" tool of your search engine to eliminate irrelevant stuff. Again, your librarian can show you how to do this.

Once you begin your library research, you may find that your question doesn't quite work. Don't be discouraged—a good question and a good literature search often evolve together. First attempts at framing a research question often turn out to be too narrow or too broad—but we can't know this until we try them out. If your question is too narrow, your searches will return too few really relevant hits. If it's too broad (which is much more likely), your searches will return too much, and sifting through page after and page of hits is neither pleasant nor productive. So learn to tweak your question as you do your research. Although it may seem like you're wasting time, spending the time to get this right in the beginning can actually save time and effort later on—and increase the chance of writing a good paper.

If you've done some smart searches and you're still not getting enough good hits, broaden your question. For example, if your question was about *drug dealers*, you might think of a more general, sociologically relevant category that might work, like *deviant identity*. Or say you decide to investigate whether Asian Americans have more stress-related health problems because of cultural pressures to excel at school—but there isn't enough published research on that exact subject. Consider whether studies on related populations, relationships, and so on could be relevant. If so, you might expand your research question beyond Asian Americans to how racial/ethnic differences in general affect stress-related illnesses.

Although you may find too few sources, you're far more likely to drown in hits when you run your first search. If you've been thoughtful about your search terms and still get pages and pages of stuff, you'll need to *narrow* your research question. Basically, this is the opposite process of what we just described. You might, say, limit your research to a particular sociodemographic group, the relationship between just two variables, the study of one geographic area, or one theoretical approach to a policy problem.

Whether you are narrowing or expanding, a good question/literature combination facilitates writing a strong library research paper—one built around questions and claims that brings sources into "conversation" with each other. Work back and forth between revising your question and searching for sources until you have a question and literature that work together: a question that can be at least roughly answered in the literature and a manageable set of articles that deals with your question in a coherent way.

Once you have your question and a good set of sources, you are ready to begin reading and writing. Much of our advice for writing literature reviews and theoretical sections of original research reports applies here as well (see pp. 96–102). The main difference is in the last part of that section: Whereas the literature review for a research paper builds up to a discussion of your own new research, the library research paper typically ends with a summary of what you've learned about your research question and perhaps a brief discussion of what still needs to be explored.

Now that we've discussed the basic concepts of getting started on a library research paper, we'll try to set you on the path to doing a first-rate one.

A Recipe for Mediocrity

At a middle school near where we live, students in the home economics class learn how to make waffles. The recipe they use isn't from a famous chef nor from an old family tradition. It's on the back of a box:

1. Beat one egg in a mixing bowl.
2. Add 2 cups of packaged waffle mix and 1 cup of milk.
3. Mix until smooth.
4. Cook on a hot waffle iron.
5. Add butter and syrup.

If this was the first thing you'd ever "cooked," both you and your teacher might have been pleased if the waffles were edible, thrilled if they were golden brown on the outside, light and fluffy on the inside. But let's not kid ourselves—displaying the culinary skill needed to make waffles from a box won't impress the manager of your local diner, much less the chef of a serious restaurant. So what does this have to do with writing a library research paper?

Tips for Writing the Library Research Paper

- *Start working with a librarian early in the process.* While getting this question/literature thing figured out isn't trivial, you don't have to go it alone. Make good use of all of those lonely librarians who desperately want you to come talk to them. If possible, find a librarian who specializes in social sciences. The librarian may not be a specialist in the area of sociology you are studying, but he will be great at maneuvering

continued

continued
around the library databases, refining searches, and teaching you new search tricks. Put that talent to work for you . . . well before the paper is due.

- *Organize your library research paper around a question or set of key questions.* One of the most common weaknesses of library research papers is a lack of *synthesis.* Students often discuss their sources one after the other, while professors want them to compare and contrast claims and evidence from their sources. The key is to organize your paper around a set of questions, not a list of sources.

- *Avoid excessive summary.* Include just enough information and detail from your sources to make your point. Keep quotations as short as possible—integrating them into your own sentences when possible.

- *Keep your voice out in front.* Start most paragraphs with ideas, points, and questions of your own. Then bring in ideas, evidence, or quotations from sources to flesh out the paragraphs.

- *Support your claims with authoritative, published evidence.* This is not the place for mere opinions—yours or others.

You've likely written many library researchers papers for school. For many of these you were asked to make an argument. In other words, the paper was supposed to present a case for your thesis (or *claim*). If, like us, you attended secondary school in the United States, you can probably remember writing such papers following a "recipe" like this:

1. Choose a thesis. (It doesn't matter whether you believe it.)
2. Find some evidence supporting your thesis. (Any evidence will do.)

3. Ignore anything that casts doubt on your thesis.
4. End paper saying that your evidence proves your claim.

We call this a "waffle mix argument"—it's a simple, fairly foolproof recipe for constructing something that meets the minimum standards. (We can all agree: that thing you have made *is* a waffle.) Yet it leads to products devoid of intelligence or inspiration: Here's my claim, here's my evidence. We're done. Let's eat. This kind of research paper might have been a reasonable expectation for secondary-school students, but . . . let's put it this way: If your sociology professor is hoping for eggs benedict with a beautifully cooked hollandaise sauce, you don't want to serve him waffles from a box. Sociology is a science; picking a claim without knowledge and then finding some evidence to support that claim is neither science nor interesting.

Embrace the Hard Questions

Even if you get off to a good start with a good question and a compelling set of sources, it's easy to fall into the trap of mediocrity. The central part of doing the research paper is synthesis: comparing and contrasting the ideas and findings of your sources. Most likely you'll likely find *some* level of agreement on *some* matters among *some* of the sources. The trap is focusing your paper on those agreements. If you do, you'll likely end up writing a coherent but short and uninteresting paper. (Source 1 says X. Sources 2, 3, and 4 basically agree. The end.) It's hard to say much of interest about simple, clear agreement. Waffles from a box.

Students are often relieved when their sources seem to clearly agree and disheartened when they conflict. But if you are striving to write a really good paper, swap these emotions. If you want to show your talent as a cook, you don't want to be judged on your ability to follow the five steps on the back of the box. Learn to see simple agreement among your sources as boring and disagreement as the sign something interesting can happen.

We're not suggesting that you should pretend agreements don't exist—just that you use them as the jumping-off point for the good stuff. Present the easy material—the obvious agreements—early in your paper. But rather than making this the focus, treat it as the background that sets up your discussion of the claims, findings, and interpretations for which you do not find clear consensus.

Your professors will be more interested in these hard questions, but they won't expect that you'll necessarily answer them. Describing where there is a lack of consensus, showing evidence of conflicting findings, and perhaps offering some possible explanations is first-rate work in itself. If your analysis suggests a plausible answer based on the evidence, by all means offer it. But a thoughtful assessment of your sources may lead you to believe that the research hasn't yet arrived at the point where meaningful conclusions can be drawn. That's a fine and rather sophisticated place to end up.

To help you better understand how to put these ideas into practice, we've made a schema for this approach. It's just a conceptual outline in three moves that you can adapt to fit your situation.

Move 1: Introduction. Topic X is interesting/important because . . . This leads to my main Question Y. Research on Question Y reveals a number of more specific questions: Y1, Y2, Y3.

Move 2: The easy stuff. For Question Y1, research to date suggests _____. Here is some typical evidence supporting this answer . . .

Move 3: The hard stuff. In contrast to Y1, the evidence for questions Y2 and Y3 is not so straightforward . . .

- For Y2: Research Z1 suggests . . . , Research Z2 says . . . , While research Z3 suggests . . .
- For Y3 . . .

Move 4: Conclusion. Look back to the issues you raised in the introduction; summarize what's clear ("research on Y1 shows . . . "), clarify what's not ("However, as I've shown, Y2 and Y3 are more complicated . . . "). Depending on what you find, you may want to end by making very specific recommendations for future research that could help resolve questions Y2, Y3, etc.

Another Approach: From Popular Press Reports to Research Literature

One of the biggest challenges in writing a library research paper is identifying an interesting but manageable question. Students usually start by trying to think up an interesting question and then beginning their research. The approach we describe here begins with a Web search, letting the Internet do some of the work of finding a question for you.

Here's the idea: Because sociology deals with human interactions, sociological research studies are frequently mentioned—and often misrepresented—in the news. An interesting and almost foolproof way to frame a library research paper is to begin with a recent story or article in the popular press that discusses a *recently published sociology-related research report*. The story then becomes your backdrop and gives you a clear research agenda: investigate the claim or claims made *about* that research in the story.

NOTE: Before trying this approach, discuss your plan with your professor to make sure it's acceptable for the assignment.

Here's a step-by-step guide to finding useful news stories or other articles about sociology research:

1. Do a Web search combining the terms *sociology, study,* and *research*, plus any particular terms related to your class, project, or topic. Let's say your class is on

sociology of the family. You might do a search with these terms using the search engine of your choice:

sociology (study OR research) (family OR parents OR siblings)

Of course, you can add other terms if you have a particular interest you'd like to pursue. For this example, you could narrow your focus by including terms such as *sibling rivalry*, *divorce*, or *grandparent*.

2. After you get your first results, click the "News" tab of your browser. This will limit your hits to news and related articles.

3. Limit your search to recent hits—perhaps the past year.

4. Look for explicit references to a specific study published recently. A quick way to find these is to open a promising hit in a new tab and then use the FIND tool to search the page for the words *study*, *research*, or *experiment*.

5. Once you find something promising, you need to locate the actual research report being discussed. If you're lucky, either the story will include a direct link to the research report, or the title of the research report will be given. If not, work from whatever information is given—usually the names of the authors and/or the name of the journal. (Your librarian can help you if you get stuck. Don't waste time here!) Open the full text in a new browser (a PDF is best) and see if the article is accessible and interesting. If so, you are ready to move on! If not, back up and try some other hits or search terms.

Our example search from step #1 turns up a number of promising hits. One of these, from the *Phys.org* website, is titled "Men more unsatisfied with extra chores in more gender equal countries":

> In countries where men and women share housework more equally, married men are more likely to be unsatisfied with their share of household duties as they report taking on a greater share of household chores, according to a new study from researchers at Emory University and Umeå University in Sweden in the journal *Social Politics*.

Using the name of the journal and key words from the title of this piece, it was easy to find the study that's being discussed: Kornrich and Eger, Family Life in Context: Men and Women's Perceptions of Fairness and Satisfaction Across Thirty Countries. *Social Politics*, Winter 2014, 21(4).

Here's another example: A number of hits from this search addressed a research report titled "Emotional Problems Among Children With Same-Sex Parents: Difference by Definition." The *Christian Post* opens its story about the study this way:

> The largest study so far on gay parenting, published this month, shows that children do best when raised by their mom and dad. While the U.S. Supreme Court has already signaled a willingness to redefine marriage to include same-sex unions for every state, it has also demonstrated a concern for how their decision will affect children.

In contrast, the *Atlantic* magazine story on the report begins like this:

> A new study claims that the children of gay couples are more likely to have emotional and developmental problems, but reveals more about the researcher than his subjects.

See the interesting tension in these two perspectives? The report was cited, in fact, by numerous other media outlets arguing either for or against same-sex parenting. This is a goldmine. Can't you imagine writing about this report—bringing it into conversation with peer-reviewed research on the topic as well as some of these other stories?

Once you have located the research report, you can easily track down more stories about that study. Just repeat steps 1–3—but add the journal name and first author's last name to the search. This should return more stories specifically about that research. This approach works best if you work from a widely read story rather than some random blog post. The former suggests that this point of view has been widely disseminated and therefore is interesting to your readers.

Look over the relevant hits and choose the story that looks most interesting. You might find more than one, which is great. If they have mostly the same take on the research, you can cite two or three of these, showing that the research was widely reported. And if they have especially different views on the research, cite (and perhaps quote from) two or more of those to explain the nature of the disagreement, what's at stake, and why it's important to look at additional research, too.

You can think about the research report plus one or more stories about that research as a library research paper kit. The stories provide both a specific research question and a context for introducing that question. You can begin your paper by introducing (and citing!) the story or stories about the research—perhaps including one or more quotations demonstrating their interest or take on the research. This will lead to a statement of *your* research agenda—which involves comparing these findings to other relevant research or theoretical work. Your analysis will focus on determining where there is consensus among the experts and where disagreement remains (refer back to the section "Embrace the Hard Questions").

A quick note about presenting "two sides of the debate": Journalists often fall into the "two-sides" trap. Finding *any* disagreement among researchers, they present them as equally plausible claims—which is misleading if one position is an outlier or from a clearly biased source. Not all social science is conducted equally well, and some researchers come to their work with a strong agenda—or even a mandate from their employer to support a particular position. (See Chapter 1 for a discussion of nonacademic research.) Present the conclusions that you think are best justified by the available evidence.

One Final Strategy for Finding a Literature: Use the Experts

Every year, an entire book of sociology literature reviews is published in a journal called the *Annual Review of Sociology.* You can think of it as a collection of truly excellent library research papers written by professional sociologists. Your professor certainly won't be expecting you to do anything nearly as extensive as these reviews, so we're not suggesting these as models for your own papers. But you can use a small part of one of these papers to find a research topic—along with references to studies on that question. Find a review that deals with a topic related to your class. Then pick out a section that seems interesting to you, and hunt within it for something you can narrow down to a research question.

For example, if you were in a course on social networks, you might look at an *Annual Review* piece that one of us wrote called "Birds of a Feather." There's a paragraph on p. 420 that's just under a subheading called "Race and Ethnicity." Just that single paragraph has citations to 10 research papers. You could first get a sense of how those papers were connected by reading the paragraph and then skim the research reports to see what looks interesting—which might lead to a question you want to pursue. Because "Birds of a Feather" was published in 2001, there will be more recent research available now. So you could use the review paragraph as a springboard—launching your investigation to learn what has been added to this knowledge base since 2001. If you based your paper on the *Annual Review* piece, you'd need to cite it, acknowledging and explaining the central role that it played in developing your paper. Again, you might want to check with your professor to make sure that this approach falls within the realm of her expectations.

As we described earlier, you'll want to write about both the agreements and unresolved questions in your own words. Be aware that a real challenge in using this *Annual Review* approach is avoiding plagiarism, making sure *your* voice comes through loud and clear in your paper. If you end up sounding too much like the original review, your professor will be more suspicious than impressed. If you want to borrow some of the language from the original review, make sure that it is clearly indicated as a quotation. (See our more extensive discussion of how to cite sources and avoid plagiarism in Chapter 8.)

STARTING YOUR ORIGINAL RESEARCH PROJECT

4

If you are undertaking an original research project of your own, you will be engaging in the same kinds of tasks that professional sociologists do when they write papers for sociology journals. Whether you are undertaking this research for your undergraduate or master's thesis, or perhaps some other capstone project, your written product will be similar to the standard sociology research report—the signature genre of sociology.

Ideally, you are reading this chapter as you begin your project. We suggest that you start by skimming Chapters 4 through 8—this will get you familiar with the various steps of the research/writing process and show you where to look in this book for guidance along the way. Because much of our advice is intended to help you make productive choices *during* the research process, you'll get more out of this book if you refer to the relevant parts as your project develops rather than waiting to read them until after your research is complete.

What Is "Research"?

Professors use the word "research" to refer to a wide variety of activities, which results in a lot of confusion.

continued

continued

Some use the terms "research paper" or "research term paper" for tasks that are quite different from the professional research report we discuss in this and the next few chapters. For those assignments, instructors typically want students to do *library research* in which they locate sources beyond the list of assigned course readings and then use those sources to discuss a concept or marshal an argument related to a course topic. We discuss this kind of assignment in Chapter 3. If you aren't sure which parts of this book relate to the task you've been assigned, ask your professor for guidance.

To help you navigate the various research-related tasks you'll need to do, we've broken the following two chapters into sections corresponding to different stages of research and analysis. These sections might be useful even if you aren't doing a full research paper. For example, the professor of your methods course may ask you to write only the Methods section for a hypothetical study. Your theory professor may assign something similar to the Literature Review and Theory section that typically follows the Introduction. Your statistics professor may give you a data set and ask you to produce the equivalent of a Results section. And in some courses, you will learn the thinking and process of sociology research through writing a *research proposal*—which involves much of the same preparation and writing as a research report but doesn't involve conducting the actual research. Different parts of Chapters 5 and 6 will be useful for these various assignments, and we'll make a few specific points about writing proposals at the end of Chapter 5 (pp. 110–112).

An Overview of the Research/Writing Process

So what are the major steps for doing a full-blown research project?

Let's start by looking at how a novice might approach a research project:

1. Come up with a topic I'm interested in.
2. Think up some way to collect some data.
3. Carry out the research.
4. Write the paper.

If you think we're critical of this plan, you're right. This novice approach often results in wasted effort, unnecessary frustration, and a lower quality result.

Here are the problems we see with this approach:

1. Starting with a *topic* rather than a *question.* "Topics" are not sufficiently focused for developing a research plan. Topics also don't make clear connections with previous lines of research. This student will struggle to write appropriate introduction and literature review sections—ones that connect her work to prior research in meaningful ways.
2. Using an arbitrary research methodology rather than one based on approaches used by other researchers. This makes it more likely that the method will turn out to be problematic. It also sacrifices the advantage of being able to justify one's method by referencing the successful work of others who've used it.
3. Treating research/writing tasks as *sequential* rather than *iterative.* Waiting to start writing late in the process deprives you of opportunities to clarify your ideas and

identify potential problems while it's still possible to deal with them productively. It also contributes to one of the biggest causes of poor research papers: running out of time.

A Note on Process

Novices think of the research process as a discrete sequence of steps. Experts approach research iteratively: they move generally forward, but often step back to rethink and adjust what they are doing along the way—especially as results start coming in. To help you understand why this difference in process matters, we'll tell you a true story about a graduate student. Let's call her Sarah.

Sarah was taking a class that required an original, potentially publishable research paper. She came up with an interesting research question: How does having a child affect a parent's obesity? She located an appropriate source of data: the Americans' Changing Lives survey (a publicly available data set). So off Sarah went—plunging forward with her research, assuming that she'd deal with the writing stuff once she'd completed her data analysis. However, when Sarah finally got around to doing the library research needed for writing the literature review part of her paper, her heart sank. Other researchers had recently published a paper on that very question using the same data set. So Sarah had to back up and find a different, related question to ask of those data. If she had *started* with a literature search, Sarah would have saved herself a lot of work. There are a lot of Sarahs.

This chapter is intended to help you go about this process intelligently. This means going back and forth between framing a question and locating the relevant literature—until you have a question asked in the right form and at the right scope to address an existing a gap in the research literature productively.

Because you are a novice sociological researcher, we are going to recommend a process that's somewhat different from what experts typically do. Because the experts have been engaged with the field for years, they are already familiar with the prior research in the area of their expertise. They know how to frame a research question that builds on an existing line of sociological inquiry. You don't. The experts also know how to choose or design a methodology that is sound and appropriate for their aims. You don't. Getting these things right before you proceed with your data collection is critical to your success, and you don't want to find out there's a problem *after* you've spent a lot of time working on your research. And one other thing: The experts can take the time they need for writing after they finish collecting and analyzing their data. You're bound by the school calendar.

For a successful research/writing process:

Don't...	Instead...
Begin with a topic.	Begin with a question.
Pick your question randomly.	Choose a question that builds on prior research.
Pick your methods randomly.	Design your methods based on what others have done studying similar kinds of questions.
Research first, then write.	Draft and revise as much as you can *as* your research proceeds. Once you have a question, you can write your Introduction. Once you are ready to begin collecting data, you can write your Methods.

So we think you'll do better, more efficient work by doing as much of the writing as you can along the way: Once you've settled on your research question, you can write a draft of the Introduction; once you've decided how to collect (or access) and analyze your data, you can take a first shot at writing Methods; and so on. The more you write along the way, the more time you'll have for getting feedback on your research *and* on your writing from your professor and peers. And you'll have time to fix what needs fixing.

In this chapter, we will help you understand how to come up with a good question that will make a contribution to that continuing conversation that is a literature. In the next chapter, we'll talk more about the basic expectations for writing about your research after you've done your analysis, and also point out the parts of the paper that you can get to work on before you even have results.

Developing a Research Question

To do sociological research, you need a sociological question. And to do good research, you need a good question. Seems simple enough, right? Yet novices frequently get tripped up at this early, critical stage. Starting with a problematic question wastes a lot of time. What would you prefer to do Saturday morning—start your research over from scratch or sleep? (Hint: choose sleep.)

OK, I need a research question . . .

Novice #1: I'll start by coming up with a question
that I think is interesting. . . . [time passes] . . .
After spending a lot of time searching, it turns

out there's no prior literature on my question.
How can I discuss the relevant literature in
the intro to my paper if there's no relevant
literature to discuss? Arrggh!

Novice #2: I'll start by finding some prior
research. I'll do a library search using a term
that I might be interested in—maybe "identity,"
"democracy," or "discrimination." . . . OK, I got
10,352 hits. What do I do now? Arrggh!

Expert: I'll start by reading some existing
research that has recently been published on a
topic that interests me. When I find one paper
that seems really intriguing, I'll figure out how
to tweak the researcher's question to take it in
a *somewhat* different direction—perhaps add
a different variable or look at a different
population. I can easily locate the relevant
literature because that's where I started!

Let's begin by stating some (often unstated) requirements for
a good research question and then unpacking them:

1. It addresses *sociological* issues.
2. It is connected to prior sociological research studies.
3. It is narrow enough that a single study can help
   answer it.
4. It can be examined through data that are already available or that you can reasonably expect to collect given
   your time and resources.

One other point: It's worth trying to choose a question
that deals with some sociology you already know something

about—perhaps from your current class or a prior one. Now, let's take these one at a time.

Is Your Question Sociological?

Not every question dealing with people or groups is a *sociological* question. Although you *can be* sociological about almost any topic, it's not automatic.

Many students approach research projects as "Sociology of Me" projects, asking questions that are important in their own lives. That may be fine, but it depends on where you plan to go from there. Say you are a student athlete, and you are annoyed that people often assume you are not intelligent because you wear a team jersey and practice every day. (We could substitute almost any category of person here . . . we all feel dissed at some point or another. Blondes are dumb. Student government officers are pretentious geeks. Professors are out of touch with current music and fashion and/or absent-minded. And so on.) So you decide to investigate "Why are people prejudiced against athletes?" That's a reasonable question and one for which suitable evidence might be found, but it's not yet a sociological question. To get there you need to generalize your personal interest—to see it as part of a broader phenomenon that applies to many situations besides your own. It's like asking a food scientist about how blue cheese spoils. He might find the question interesting in the abstract, but he doesn't care about the block of Roquefort that you just found in your refrigerator.

There's another potential problem with "Sociology of Me" projects: When students do field research for such projects, they often want to interact with people who are a lot like them—maybe even their friends. That's understandable; it's much more comfortable than talking to people who are really different from you. But the chances of learning something interesting from interviewing people much like you are pretty slim.

To avoid this narrow, self-centered approach, begin by thinking about sociological concepts that could be a lens through which to view your specific concern. "Student athlete" is a category of people, a social position, right? So you are interested in how people associate characteristics with categories of people. You might recall a class lecture about or reading about "stereotypes" or "identity meanings"—or even "ideologies" if you're talking about big, politically loaded categories. You're off to a promising start now. Few people are student athletes, but almost everyone is or has been in a category of people that is associated with negative characteristics.

As a novice, you'll probably be surprised to know that whether sociologists (e.g., your professors) find a question interesting depends more on whether it's clearly connected to current theory or policy issues rather than something interesting about the topic itself. *You* might want to study whether first-year students at your school from New York or Alabama are more likely to shake hands or fist bump when they meet another student, but few sociologists would care. But if you can relate that question to how cultural forms of interaction spread through social networks, you might be on to something promising.

How to Make a Question "Sociological"

- Pose a question that is interesting at two different levels—at an abstract theoretical level *and* at a concrete, vivid level of specific cases or incidents.
- Find a theory (or two) that should apply to the phenomenon in which you are interested. What type of evidence could help you decide whether the theory works in that context?

By all means, choose a topic that interests you. But then transform the topic into a sociological question. The surest way to accomplish this is to find a published study that relates to your question and then build on that. If a study has been published in a peer-reviewed journal, you know that at least the editor and reviewers found it sociologically important. It contributed to a literature, so your follow-up study would, too. So, let's see where that strategy leads us.

The Problem with Novelty

As we've said, novelty for its own sake makes it hard to do an essential part of sociology research writing—discussing how the new research relates to prior work. If no one has done any related prior work . . . well, you see the problem. However, you should pay close attention to your specific assignment. Sometimes a professor wants you to try your hand at collecting and analyzing data to learn about methods and presenting evidence. In that case, she might tell you just to pick a question you are curious about with no expectation that you will connect your project to a literature. This is different from doing "real" sociological research, so it may be fine to choose a question that is just novel and interesting. But make sure!

Novelty works against you in ways other than just limiting the relevant literature you'll find. Don't underestimate how convenient it is to use measures developed by someone else to study the thing you are interested in. Measuring sociological variables is difficult, so picking up a measure that someone else figured out for her research is a safer bet than coming up with your own measures. The earlier researchers had to keep refining that measure until it generated results worth publishing. Students often think they score points for inventing new ways of doing things. Their professors see more value in adapting an existing method referenced in a peer-reviewed paper. It shows that you've been reading (and paying attention). It also gives you one very direct connection to prior research. Now let's look at some other ways to make that connection.

Does Your Question Connect to Prior Research?

To be meaningful sociological research, your work must contribute to a cumulative body of scientific knowledge. You won't be expected to publish your research for a class assignment (although it can happen: an undergraduate in one of our departments got a book contract based on her honors paper showing how and when Asian American students developed romantic relationships with non-Asians). However, you *will* be expected to show how your work builds on what others have done before you.

You might now be thinking, "So I can only do what other people have already done? How unoriginal and uninteresting." But it's not. Someone once said, "Yes, you think that the sun orbits around the earth. And that *is* what it looks like, given the way you're looking at it. But I have a different way to think about it." You can make that study about fist bumping an important, interesting piece of sociological work. You just have to figure out a way to connect it to something that sociologists have studied before. You can build on the literature. You can challenge it. But to ignore it means you're not doing science, which is a cumulative enterprise developed by lots of people cooperating and competing. That's the big "conversation" you're trying to work your way into.

A good strategy is to start by finding a research report in which someone investigated something you are interested in—or something fairly close—and then extending his or her work in some way. In fact, it's easier to *start* with a study or a theory that engages your interest than to start with the broad question, "What am I interested in?" Perhaps you can remember a piece of research that got your attention when you read it for a course, or was cited in something that you read, or that your professor talked about in class. Building from a specific text might be easier than starting with a specific personal concern ("Why do people think I'm not smart because I'm an athlete?" or "Why do people from New Jersey fist bump?") and then trying to relate that to a general, abstract sociological issue. Library research on personal topics will also get you a lot of junk (things that aren't sociology). Try a Web search for "student athlete" or "fist bump" and you'll see what we mean: You'll get lots of hits, but not much on status characteristics theory, negative stereotypes, or network diffusion that would help you develop a great paper.

From Existing Research to a New Project

Let's assume you're taking our advice and you have found a research article that interests you. How might you expand it to do something new *enough*, hitting that sweet spot between complete novelty and boring repetition? Here are some options that might work. But before settling on one, be sure to check with your professor. What is acceptable depends on what the assignment is trying to teach or assess. For example, if you're expected to develop a research method, the first two options might not fit.

1. You might do a replication. That seems like the least original thing possible. But remember that replication is the core of science—the idea is that someone else observing the same thing under (roughly) the same conditions will see the same thing. Now, whatever research you are reading, you can be sure that you can't do *exactly* the same thing. You are a different person, at a different time, in a different setting. So even trying to do what the author(s) did would be an extension of sorts. If the prior study used data from a major national survey in 2000 and you replicate it in another high-quality national data set from

2015, you are doing a replication, but at a different time period. If your results confirm theirs, it would show that their findings still hold today. (Unless the later survey happens to use exactly the same measures, those might vary, too. That would show that the results weren't based on just one way of measuring the thing of interest.)

2. The next extension goes a little farther—choosing to intentionally vary the research setting. Does the author's finding in X population hold for Y population? You might find a study about "hooking up" for short sexual relationships at a large public university in the South (Lambert et al. 2003) and wonder whether the findings would be the same in a small, elite private school on the West Coast. Those are very different environments. You might have a theoretical argument and a hypothesis about how the different school size, student diversity, or cultural scene might affect the results. The nice thing about this approach is that you have an interesting finding either way: If the same pattern *does* hold up in the very different environment, you've got a strong replication. If you find differences, you've got something interesting to explain to your reader. Either way, you don't have to do the basic design of the study—it's already been done.

3. You could ask the same question as that in the report but use a different specific case to answer it. Say the article that interests you showed that Mexican children of highly educated indigenous parents were more likely to self-identify as indigenous themselves, compared with children of less educated indigenous parents (Villereal 2014). You could look at the concepts that were studied in that article, and try to figure out how to study those same concepts with a different type of data. In this example, the important relationship is between indigenous identification and parental education. The fact that this

paper examined identification as an indigenous Mexican was just their specific case. You might ask whether this might be true of immigrants from other countries. (You might be able to use existing survey data to answer that question, or you could design your own survey for students at your school.)

4. Another option is to add a new element—perhaps by changing the independent or dependent variable. The study of Mexican indigenous identification focused on the education level of the parents. Maybe you think that the composition of the neighborhood might also be a factor. If the study you are working from used publicly available data, you could get the data set and add the new independent (explanatory) variable that you are interested in to the analysis. That way you have both a replication *and* something new to talk about.

5. You could also change the method used to investigate a published research question. Suppose that you read Jessi Streib's (2015) book on marriages that cross social class lines in your stratification class. You won't have the years that it took her to do the in-depth interviews and qualitative analysis that were her evidence. But you could do a targeted survey of cross-class romances on your own campus, asking questions about the issues that Streib found to cause class-based conflicts.

The most difficult approach to developing a research paper might be starting with a general theoretical question and translating it into a specific researchable question. Why is this so hard? Because you've got to do everything yourself. First, you've got to identify the main concepts. Say you are reading a work on organizational ecology theory for your Organizations course. There are a lot of concepts floating around in the reading, but your attention is drawn to two: "size" and "differentiation." The theory makes an argument that these two things—both important for organizational performance—are related. You're well on your way: You've identified the main concepts and how the theory argues that they are connected. Now you've got to figure out for yourself how to measure these things in a research setting. That can be a complicated task in itself. For example, since you have access to campus organizations, perhaps you decide to study those. Determining each organization's size is pretty straightforward—how many members do they have? But how will you measure differentiation? Most of the articles you read are talking about businesses, measuring differentiation with the number of divisions in companies or the range of products they sell. That doesn't have anything to do with campus organizations. You will have to think up a new way to measure differentiation in this new setting.

Starting from theory requires more thought, creativity, work, and patience than options 1–5 from earlier. But it can be very rewarding. Just be sure to work through the process systematically and consult with your professor before you actually begin collecting data—to make sure that your measures really get at the concepts you want to study. Be sure to pay attention to how scientists in your theoretical tradition have typically measured things in their studies. That can be an important lead.

A Word About Novelty

You might believe that a good research question is one that no one has yet thought to ask. But as a newcomer to the field, how can you know what questions *have* already been asked?

continued

continued

Novelty doesn't make a question worth answering. In fact, if it's not directly related to research that's already been done, there's likely an unforeseen roadblock ahead. Rather than worrying about novelty, build on what others have done. That's science. When you search for things on Google Scholar, you'll see that the opening page has a quote from Robert K. Merton about "standing on the shoulders of giants." Merton was a sociologist—a great one—and the father of a Nobel Prize winner. If he was willing to build on the works of others, it's okay for you as well.

You are learning to do what's called "normal science" as a novice. Once you know how to complete a well-formed research process, you might be able to break out into more novel ideas that might transform the field. But following the lead of others is a much higher payoff strategy at first.

Is Your Question Narrow Enough?

Novice researchers typically choose questions that are much, much broader than what an expert would choose, and the experts aren't limited by the time constraints of semesters. A common cause of insufficiently focused questions is mistaking a *topic* for a *question*. A professional sociologist could take a typical student research topic and slice it up into 50 perfectly good research questions. Your professor may have spent her entire career studying something narrower than your first idea for your paper.

Say you've noticed that people at your campus drink alcohol a lot, and that they seem especially likely to get drunk when they are out with other people who are drinking a lot. This pattern gives you an idea for your research project, which you frame sociologically: "I'm going to study peer influence on drinking." Is that narrow enough? With a bit of database work you locate a review article on the subject (Borsari and Carrey 2001). It was written over 10 years ago and has citations for around 100 research studies. (There have been hundreds more done since then.) Every one of these studies represents a separate research project on the topic of peer influence on drinking. Do you get our point?

In the face of so much existing research, the novice might worry that everything worth doing has already been done. The expert, on the other hand, sees every study as a source of new questions. Let's imagine you begin your search for a research question with this article: "Peer Influences: The Impact of Online and Offline Friendship Networks on Adolescent Smoking and Alcohol Use," published in the *Journal of Adolescent Health*. In this study (Huang et al. 2014), a large survey of 10th graders in Southern California revealed that using social network sites didn't have much influence on drinking behavior, but getting photographs of drinking parties from their friends did. How might you develop a new research question from this article?

Here are some options:

- *Change with age*: "Are older students differently affected by this kind of peer influence than younger students?" You have college students around you—maybe you could survey them. Or maybe you could find a data set (like Add-Health) that has younger students.
- *Change over time*: "Does peer influence affect students differently today than in the past?" Maybe you could find an older data set to compare with the findings of Huang and colleagues. Or maybe you could find something recent about social network use or smartphone apps that didn't

exist when the earlier study was done, and compare that with their results.

- *Difference by gender*: "Does the sharing of pictures of alcohol consumption at parties affect men and women differently?" Because it's a common belief that men and women use Web resources differently, you could probably find some literature to suggest this idea. The original article controlled for gender, but it didn't focus on it. You could do so, by thinking about it more deeply and looking for statistical interactions between gender and the main independent variable (sharing pictures).

- *Difference by race, ethnicity, sexual preference, region, or religion*: Because the Huang study was done in Southern California, it had a particular sociodemographic setting. If you did a study in the US South, for example, you'd have a much larger group of African Americans and non-Hispanic Whites (who made up only .4 percent and 4.9 percent of the Huang sample, respectively). For that matter, being Latino would have a different *meaning* in areas where that group isn't so large. (Almost 70 percent of this sample was Hispanic.)

- *Difference by socioeconomic background*: This study was done in one school district, so it didn't have much variation in socioeconomic status. Another data set might have more variation.

- *Difference by group membership*: You might ask whether drinking by Greeks (sorority and fraternity members) affected more or less by peers than non-Greeks. If you shift to a new population (like college students), new group memberships might become relevant. Greek affiliation didn't appear in this study of predominantly Hispanic schools, but it might be central in a study of college students' response to social media.

- *Focusing on a particular range of the dependent variable*: While looking for this paper, we found another paper that argued that heavy drinking had different sources than lighter drinking. Studying the impact of social media on binge drinking (versus having one or two drinks) might be interesting.

- *Adding a new variable*: There's a literature that shows that family members have a lot of influence on drinking behavior. Adding this variable to the mix might be interesting, especially if you use college students. Does family influence continue into the college years?

By developing your question directly from an earlier paper, you already have a pretty good review of the literature up until then (that's what the peer review process gets you; the authors have already gotten an "A" on their paper by getting it published). You can check the papers that cite your core paper to add more recent things (more about that later). And by focusing on just one new element, you both cut down the relevant literature (a lot!) and give yourself something specific to examine.

Can You Get the Data You Need in the Time You Have?

When students think about doing research, they often think first about collecting data by talking to people: They want to interview other people (usually other students) about something. In some courses, especially methods courses, you might not have a choice about whether to do a quantitative or qualitative study. But for some assignments, you will.

Qualitative research—whether based on interviews or careful ethnographic observations—might *seem* easier than working with quantitative data, because you avoid the "s-word" (statistics). But the truth is that it's seriously hard work, and it can take lots of time—not just to do the interviewing or observation, but to transcribe and code the interviews, and to analyze and interpret the information after you get it. Let's do a little math: It might take half an hour to recruit and schedule each interview, the same or more to do each interview (plus travel time), then several hours to transcribe and code the conversation: that's 5 or 6 hours for every interview you do. Probably 10 interviews would be a bare minimum for learning anything systematic. (You should ask your professor what would be acceptable here.) Allow for a little bad luck along the way (that happens in research), and that means you'll need to put in a couple of full-time work weeks before you've even started any real analysis or writing of results.

We don't want to imply that you should avoid qualitative research. We just want to make sure you aren't mistakenly imagining it to be easier or faster than doing a quantitative project of equal quality. Qualitative studies might also involve some expenses for things like transcribing or coding software. If you're thinking about gathering qualitative data, be sure to talk to your professor early about the level of evidence that will be acceptable, and whether your plans are realistic.

Because gathering data in sufficient quantities is challenging even for experts, professional sociologists often work with data that's already available in the form of databases. If you have a choice of methods, consider working from databases—especially if your project is limited to a single semester. There are some really big repositories of data that have been collected by social scientists over many years. The biggest one is probably the ICPSR—the Inter-University for Political and Social Research   (https://www.icpsr.umich.edu/icpsrweb/landing.jsp). They've collected data sets about all sorts of things. Although most of these data are surveys, there are some text files and interview transcripts as well. This means you could use these data to do either quantitative or qualitative studies.

Working with one of these previously collected databases has an additional benefit beyond access to high-quality data: You almost always get a literature to go with it. If someone went to the trouble to collect data on a topic, he or she almost always published something out of it. So you can both look at what people measured and at what people have published using these data to date.

For example, if you're interested in the IPCSR category "Conflict, Aggression, Violence, Wars," you can search and choose between "Conflict and Stability Within Nations" and "Conflict Between and Among Nations." If you choose the latter, you'll find African Coup Events Data, 1986–1990 (ICPSR 6869) collected by T. Y. Wang. You can then search on both the data set and the author using Google Scholar or some other search engine: There you have a starting literature and some specific papers from which you could develop a research project. In fact, ICPSR makes this even easier for you by including some key citations that use the data right in the data listing! One of those could become your core article or book for developing your study. In short, you could be studying African coups within a few hours, all while sitting on your couch. What a wonderful social scientific world it is!

"Database" Confusion

In sociology, *database* can mean two very different things. Because both meanings relate to research work, there's potential for confusion.

> *Meaning #1*: a collection of previously collected data available for new analyses. Many sociological studies are analyses of data selected from such sets, because researchers can rarely gather such a large quantity of high-quality data on their own.

continued

> *Meaning #2*: an online, searchable index of published work—accessible through university library websites. Although some databases are general (Web of Science), sociologists often work with those specifically intended for the social sciences like Sociological Abstracts or JSTOR.

Here are more examples of first-rate databases. (There are lots of others, too.)

- American National Election Survey (http://www.election studies.org/). Studied every Presidential election since the mid-1950s using interviews before and after the election.
- General Social Survey (http://www3.norc.org/GSS+ Website/). Interviewed a probability sample of US adults every couple of years since the 1970s.
- Survey Documentation and Analysis project (http://sda .berkeley.edu/). Out of University of California-Berkeley, it contains both the American National Election Surveys and the General Social Survey, as well as a lot of US Census data and some more specialized studies. This site also provides a set of nice analysis tools as well, if you want to do your analysis without learning new software.

Other databases are so big that they have their own websites to show you how to download and use the data. Here are some good examples:

- National Longitudinal Study of Adolescent Health (Add Health)
- National Study of Youth and Religion (NSYR)

- National Study of the Changing Workforce (NSCW)
- World Values Survey (WVS)
- International Social Survey Programme (ISSP)

If you read about a database in a published article and are thinking about using it for your research, do a Web search for the database name. You'll often find a site that tells you how you can use the data to do related research. If you are an international student, you might be able to find data sets in languages other than English. You could also choose to contrast a country of which you have specialized knowledge in the World Values Survey or the International Social Survey to the United States.

Every question in these data sets is "sociologically important" in some real sense. Groups of social scientists decided that each question was worth an investment, because collecting data costs real money. (The usual rule at the General Social Survey is 15 seconds for respondents to answer a simple, straightforward, fixed-choice question; this doesn't sound like much until you realize it costs around $25,000 to ask it.). A skilled sociologist can literally pick almost any two questions from one of these big data sets and create a good research project—and the evidence is already there! (No, our actual work is not nearly that arbitrary.) So, consider the publicly available data option when you are given a research project—unless the assignment specifies that you collect data yourself, which could be the case if your professor wants you to learn how to do your own data collection.

Don't Let Big Databases Scare You Off

It can be overwhelming at first to look at publicly available data sources—there are so many variables and

continued

continued

so many publications out of them. But don't be discouraged. They are an incredible resource—and learning how to use such databases is less work and more dependable than collecting your own data. And don't worry that using these big data sets might require statistical analysis. Someone can help guide you through the process. Professors know that students never *really* learn statistics until they do it for themselves. (Remember, they were students once, too.) They won't be surprised that you need a little refreshing.

People at your school can help you with the practical issues of downloading the data, too. There are often "help desks" on campus that are designed for just this purpose. You could even go back to the professors that taught you statistics in the first place for help. They'll probably be pleased to see that you are using the skills that you learned in their courses.

Finding a Literature

Here's the bad news: Students often spend too much time on library research and still get unsatisfactory results. Here's the good news: Others can do some of this work for you—or, rather, *with* you. We're not sure why, but it seems oddly difficult to convince students to get help with their literature searches from the very people their school *pays* to help them: librarians.

For novices like yourself, there are two distinct challenges involved in doing a good literature search: understanding what "a literature" is and understanding what constitutes well-chosen sources. Once you grasp these concepts, you should be able to do a high-quality search with a librarian's assistance in a fraction of the time you're likely to spend on your own.

(There's a lot more information about this in Chapter 7 on "Choosing and Using Sources.")

What Is "a Literature"?

You should know that this was a hard question even for *us* to answer. It's a serious case of "implicit knowledge"—things that people know but find it hard to communicate to others. It's like explaining the difference between a big house and a mansion to a five-year-old . . . or explaining the difference between Instagram and Snapchat to one of us!

Let's go back to that image of research from Chapter 1: a big party with lots of people. Everyone isn't in one big conversation; they are grouped in clusters. The discipline is like the party, and the conversational clusters are like the literatures. So we've got to figure out the boundaries of *your* conversation.

You can think of this as a network problem. What are the parts of social science that cluster together? If we start at the biggest level, we see disciplines: Economists talking to economists, and political scientists talking to political scientists. But we are talking about a much more fine-grained view when we're looking for a literature. Who is talking about the question you want to answer? How can you use what they have done and what they are saying to help you think about your own research?

If you haven't yet found that "core article" we recommended earlier, you might start with a research source from one of your classes. If you're a graduate student, you're reading articles in your seminars. If you are an undergraduate, look at your texts; all undergraduate textbooks build on existing research. Go to one of their citations that looks like a research report. That's probably a core piece of research. We're trying to get you to think about research that you've been reading about in class in a different way. The first time through your focus was on what the authors learned. But now you want to think about this article or book as a research endeavor: What did they do? Whose work were they building on? You need to find the interrelated set of articles that are talking about the same thing, in the same way.

Maybe it helps to think of finding a literature as analogous to finding that group of students on your campus who share one of your interests. If you're into doubles table tennis, who tends to organize and play pick-up games on the weekend? You want to "find" the cluster of sociologists that are studying the same questions in ways that allow them to talk to one another—and you want to play, too. You should plan to explore a few of those clusters before you hit on the right research question and literature. Getting *this* part of the research process right will make everything else much, much easier.

Library Databases: The Professional Resource for Finding Sources

University libraries are different from public libraries. They are focused on the work of supporting research. One of the most valuable features of your university library website is access to research databases. Your school's library will likely have dozens, if not over a hundred, different specialized databases—each designed to facilitate finding the best sources for some research area. Your librarians will be happy to guide you in choosing the best database for your project and even teach you how to use it effectively.

The last decade has brought about a powerful new database feature: the ability to search *forward* in time from when an article was published to see who cited it. Two excellent databases for this are Web of Science/Web of Knowledge and JSTOR. Ask you librarian to show you how to use this feature to find more good sources once you've found one.

What Is an Appropriate Source?

If you search the Internet for a sociological topic, you'll find lots of stuff. Top on the list might be a Wikipedia article. That's not a bad thing. It means you've chosen a topic that people were interested enough in to write an entry about. You should recognize that Wikipedia articles aren't serious academic texts, although they can be fine as a launch pad. If the article is any good, it will cite some core sources. (If it doesn't, ignore it; it clearly wasn't written by a scientist.) Look up some of those sources. Once you find a single, high-quality, very relevant reference—your "core" source for this process—use the Web of Science database to look both forward and backward in time for more sources: What references did your core paper cite? Who cited your core source? The date of an article will give you a clue about which direction to focus on. If it was published in the last year or two, look backward at their citations and see what they are building on. If it's an older piece, look forward to see who has cited your core article. Things that are cited often are usually more important than things that are rarely cited. (Web of Science gives you this "score" automatically). Even being cited a few times is an indicator that an article is getting attention.

Once you begin your search, don't start reading your hits immediately. You want to be efficient and read only those articles that are likely to contribute to your project. Once you have your hits, scan the titles. If something looks promising, skim the abstract. If you get no good hits, or only a couple, that's a sign that you may need to reframe your question. But if even a dozen or so hit the target of your topic, you are looking at a stream of thought you can build on.

If this all seems daunting, remember our earlier advice: Do this with a librarian. And do it early. This is not a task for the week before your paper is due. This is a task that begins *before* you settle on a research question. In fact, this reading will help you formulate an effective one. The search for a literature and the development of a research question are very much a chicken-and-egg thing: Work back and forth between the two processes until they fit together.

Basically, you are trying to find the articles that are the *core* of the social scientific literature about your topic. For a serious research project, shoot for a minimum of 15. Without at least 10 or so, you won't have enough material to build on—a weak foundation. But for a class project that must be completed in less than a semester, many more than that will leave you without enough time to deal seriously with any of them. A list of 50 sources will be like having a tractor-trailer load of random building materials dumped on a construction site; even if what you need is there, you don't have time to sift through piles of lumber to find a doorknob.

You might be wondering how can we say how many sources you'll need without knowing your research question? It's a matter of how wide to cast your net. If the sea in front of you is teeming with sea life (think peer effects on drinking), then you have to decide what you want to catch. If you fish in one spot for an hour and get only a couple of nibbles (think of the impact of taking sociology courses on beliefs about poverty), then you need to move around a bit more.

The Path to Skeptical Enlightenment

When students begin to seriously examine sociology research literature, they tend to read at one of two extremes. Initially, they assume that because it's "science," and because it got published, everything in it *must* be "true." This is our *gullible* stage in Figure 4.1. But then, as students begin to learn about the methods of sociology, they discover that things like the wording of a survey question or the way data are coded can have a big effect on the evidence that gets collected. They learn that

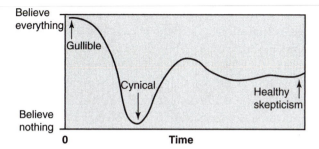

FIGURE 4.1 The path from gullibility through cynicism to enlightenment—a healthy skepticism.

databases can be mined for different things in different ways, and they see examples in their statistics class of standard techniques being used incorrectly. And they hear their professors point out the limitations of research reports that they have read. These students may now enter the *cynical* stage, in which they see all sociology research as inherently flawed and thus worthless. Students at this stage risk doing what your grandmother might have referred to as "throwing the baby out with the bathwater."

We hope you will get through these naive stages quickly and move on to the more mature and useful stage of *healthy skepticism*. The skeptical reader understands that any piece of sociology research might be misleading—whether because of improperly applied methods, overgeneralized claims, or other limitations or flaws. Yet she is also careful to read *generously*— understanding that despite any limitations, the research can help us understand some aspect of the social world better than we could if that research hadn't been published. Without such generosity we are left with neither baby nor bathwater, only a dirty tub, puddles of water, wet toilet paper, and an assortment of now purposeless squeaky rubber toys. Think about it.

The objective is to avoid cynical readings—in which you dismiss entire studies outright because of imperfections—while maintaining the critical stance you need to be a smart consumer of sociological research. Once you start doing research of your own, you will get more generous still; you'll learn how hard it is to conduct even a decent study, and that there are trade-offs for each decision you make.

A Suggestion About Process

Students often end up with a pile of printed papers (often with lots of highlighting), but few ideas about how to use them. It's actually hard to remember the key points that you got out of a research article even a day or two after you read it. So how are you going to bring it back up to the surface a few *weeks* later, when you are writing your literature review or theory section? When you find an article that is worth reading all of the way through (in other words, one that is really useful and central to your research question and its literature), you might take notes on a sort of duel ledger. On one side, make note of the important arguments or findings that the paper makes. On the other, make notes to yourself about how you might *use* that information in constructing your own argument. You can do something similar by inserting comments in Word or PDF files. Or, if you want to get really sophisticated (and efficient), learn how to take notes using a reference manager tool like Endnote, RefWorks, Mendeley, or Zotero.

Don't make either of these ledgers voluminous repetitions of what's actually in the article itself. After all, if you find that you need more detail when you are actually drafting your paper, the article will still be there to go back and read. Instead, just hit the biggest, most useful points, and make a note to yourself about how you might use them. Then you'll be able to reconstruct your thought process while you were reading, even if some time has passed.

Establishing a Theoretical Framework

To make your research truly sociological, you'll need to relate it to a general theoretical framework that's been developed in the field. Like the question and the literature review, this process is a chicken-and-egg problem. Which theory or theories you use will depend on your question . . . but your question might be driven by the developments in some theory that you have studied in class (or read about in your literature review). When you see authors mentioning the same old texts to frame their work, substitute "classic" for "old" in your mind. Often these are the works that underpin the entire area. Although it may seem inefficient to go back and read something that is decades old, it might be exactly what you need to provide a theoretical framework for your paper.

Don't hesitate to ask your professor (or another in your department) for some guidance in identifying relevant theory. Your professors will be even more likely than a librarian to know a source that gives a good, classic overview of a theoretical perspective. What if you are offered more than one theoretical perspective? Sometimes an area of research is characterized by two competing theories. Then you have a decision to make. Are you going to have the ability to say whether one or the other is best able to describe your evidence? Or should you make a decision early on to use just one of the approaches to the question? Again, a professor's advice can help here.

Even if the conversation that you are joining is not very theoretical (it doesn't talk about these classic sources), you'll need to consider the *processes* (we often call them "mechanisms") that link the variables in your research question. So, when you are exploring that literature, spend some time thinking about *why* X would be related to Y. Look for some studies on that topic as well. They will be useful as you start to draft the early parts of your paper . . . which we discuss in the next chapter.

5

WRITING ABOUT YOUR ORIGINAL RESEARCH: *BEFORE* YOU HAVE DATA

So you've taken the time to develop an interesting and manageable research question. You have made certain that your question is situated within the existing research literature. You have identified a theoretical framework. Congratulations— it's time to get moving on your research! But don't make the common mistake of waiting to begin writing your paper until you have completed your research. Writing as you go helps you think critically about your project as you go. It also gives you time to get feedback on your research while there is time to make needed adjustments. You can make sure you have a good question and a meaningful theoretical framework by getting feedback on a draft of your Introduction *before* you start figuring out your methods. And by getting feedback on a rough draft of your Methods section, you can make sure your methods are sound *before* you begin collecting data.

And that's not all: starting the writing early lets you do your best writing because you're not in a panic. And believe us, if you wait to write the entire paper until after you've collected and analyzed your data, you will likely be pushing your deadline just to write a *complete* report—much less an excellent one. Finally, it gives you the time to follow a writing process that is most likely to be successful. Spreading the writing out over time gives you opportunities to revise your work in response to feedback. Just as important, it gives you the chance to step away from your writing for a few days and come back to it with fresh eyes. Honestly, even if you spend the same total amount of time on the writing, spreading that time out over a few weeks or months will result in better science and a much better written product.

What Is a Research Report?

To write a first-rate research report, you need to understand what you are trying to produce. The main purpose of a research report is to present the methods and findings of newly conducted research to other researchers, and by doing so advance knowledge in the field. Writing a research report involves explaining *why* you did the research, *how* you did it, *what* you found, and *what* those findings mean. Although particulars will vary, any full-blown research report you write should do these things:

1. Tell readers what your research question is and explain why it's worth trying to answer it. (Introduction)
2. Show readers how your research relates to prior work in the field and with existing theory. (Literature Review/ Theory)
3. Convince readers that your evidence was collected and analyzed appropriately. (Methods)
4. Present your findings. (Results)
5. Interpret your findings in relation to the question and the prior literature. (Discussion)

These five tasks shape the genre of the research report. Although the amount of space needed to accomplish each task depends on many factors, we know it's difficult to write with no sense of expected length. So in the following table, we've

Who Are You Writing For?

Students often have difficulty deciding what needs explaining and how much detail to include. That's to be expected if you don't have a good sense of your audience. Unless you've been told otherwise, use these guidelines: Assume your readers have a general knowledge of sociology, but don't assume they know much about the *subfield* of your research. And definitely don't assume they have any prior knowledge about your particular project. Even if your only reader will be your instructor (who you should be talking to frequently), write for a smart, social-science-literate reader who has not heard about your project before.

estimated the length for each part of the report (in double-spaced text). We've based these estimates on the typical journal article This should be about right for a capstone undergraduate or major graduate research paper. If you are doing a one-semester project and your teacher tells you to aim for something shorter, you might cut our estimates. If your department has a tradition of longer theses (you *have* looked at good models, right?), you can multiply up, but keep the same rough proportions.

Although most of the parts listed in the table clearly have different jobs to do, novice research writers are often confused by the repetition that occurs: The Abstract tells your reader something about the literature and theory you are building on, states your research question, and summarizes both your method of collecting evidence and what you found—all in about 250 or 300 words. Then your Introduction does much of this again (perhaps leaving out the results) in a couple of pages.

Parts of the Typical Research Paper

Section	Purpose	Typical Length
Title Page	Gives basic identifying information.	1 page
Abstract	Summarizes the research, including the research question, the theoretical approach, and the key findings.	1/2 page
Introduction	Introduces the topic and prior relevant research. Shows how the new research adds to what has been done.	1–2 pages
Literature Review and Theory	Describes the literature in more detail. Reviews the theoretical process that could generate an answer to your question. Suggests hypotheses for the answer to your question.	5–7 pages
Methods	Describes *who* you are studying, *what* measures or techniques you used, and *how* you collected and analyzed your data.	2–4 pages
Results	Presents the analysis of your data. If you explicitly stated your hypotheses, states which were supported or rejected.	4–8 pages
Discussion and Conclusion	Connects your analyses back to your research question. States the limitations of your study. Suggests ideas for future research.	2–3 pages
References	Lists full citations for all sources mentioned.	As needed
Appendices (Optional)	Presents other important materials, such as complete questionnaires, interview guides, or stimuli; IRB protocol; lists of descriptive information about your variables if too lengthy to put in results; analyses that support your conclusions but that weren't central enough to make the main paper.	As needed

Then your Literature Review and Theory sections elaborate yet again on parts of the Introduction. Why all the redundancy?

It has to do with how experts read research reports. Think back to how *you* used research papers during your own literature search while you were formulating your research question. Remember how you scanned titles and then the abstracts to see if a paper was relevant to your question? You needed the basic information in that short form to help you decide whether to even read any of the paper. If things looked promising, then you started to skim the paper from the beginning. The expert reader does something similar.

When the expert decides to read the article, *how* she reads depends on her relationship to the paper. If it's in her area of expertise, she might be familiar with the related literature and theory—in which case she'll jump from the Introduction straight to the Methods . . . or perhaps go next to the Results. These readers may not even read the Results in order—often skipping straight to the tables and figures to get their own take on the evidence. On the other hand, if the reader is less familiar with this line of research, she may take the time to read the entire Literature Review section. The Introduction, then, needs to give an overview of the paper that works for a variety of readers, giving them a "road map" of the argument that the paper will make. So the Abstract, Introduction, and body of the paper really *do* repeat some material—but at different levels of detail to accommodate how different audiences are likely to read.

Writing Introductions

Once you've settled on a question and identified a literature, there's no reason *not* to write a draft of the Introduction. You may be wondering, "How do I introduce my research when I don't even know my results yet?" Fair question—especially since your professors probably don't write their introductions until later in the process. So, why do we want you to do it now? Because there is a real difference between how experts and novices do their best work.

The expert sociologist will already be familiar with the research literature and the important questions that should be asked next. It's mostly a matter of finding the time and money to do the research and write it up for publication. (Ask your professor about research ideas that are percolating in his or her head. Professors typically have many more good research ideas than time to carry them out. They'd love for you to pick up one of these and do a research paper on it. We call it mentorship.) But finding a literature, forming a question, and figuring out what kind of evidence can answer it is a learned skill.

As a novice researcher, we suggest that you write a first draft of an introduction as soon as possible. You'll undoubtedly need to rewrite this introduction before the paper is finally done: your question may shift based on what you find along the way, you might find other literature or a different theoretical perspective to include, and so on. But writing down the basic idea at the beginning means that you will know where you're headed; it also gives you something to share with your professor early in the process to make sure you are on the right track. So, although experts might not start with their introductions, we think that you should.

When people read a literary essay, they appreciate interesting, even innovative, beginnings. But those who read research reports or research proposals in sociology prefer a more consistent way of starting—one that presents the intentions of the new project systematically, explaining how the new research builds on, and perhaps challenges, prior theory and research. We can understand how the typical introduction is structured if we think of it in terms of *moves* that authors make. Four such moves are commonly used in writing research report introductions:

Move 1: State your research topic and explain its importance.

Move 2: Give an overview of the most important and relevant research that has already been done. Describe the theory or theories that drive that research.

Move 3: Explain what's new about your research in relation to the research you discussed in Move 2. (We call this establishing the research "gap.")

Move 4: Say how your research helps to fill that gap.

Here is an example of an introduction from a brief research report published in *American Sociological Review*. Note how readers are alerted to each move by a word or phrase (shown in boldface type).

Introduction

Recent research in racial stratification has become increasingly sensitive to the substantial—and apparently growing—economic heterogeneity within the black population. No longer is the black population treated as a monolithic whole or in stereotypical terms. **Studies of** class polarization within the black community (Farley 1984), of the growing black middle class (Landry 1987), and of the chronic problems of the black "underclass" (Wilson 1980, 1987) give ample testimony to this fact. **Nevertheless,** spatial heterogeneity in the black population **continues to be**

#1 State the research topic

#2 Summarize previous research

#3 Describe the gap

largely ignored, despite apparent evidence of rather striking differences in black socio-economic status from city to city (Farley 1988). **Current debates have focused largely on** the changing status of urban blacks, while excluding nonmetropolitan blacks (see Wilson 1987; Farley 1988). Unfortunately, rural blacks today are more spatially dispersed than urban blacks, less visible, and apparently easier to ignore. **The main objective of this study is** to examine patterns of black employment-related hardship and racial inequality in the nonmetropolitan South.

#3 continued

#4 Introduce your research

Writers of effective introductions recognize that sociologists are more interested in research *progress* than novelty. Rather than dazzling readers with your originality, you want to show how your research sheds new light on a relevant sociological issue, concept, or theory.

In this unusually brief example, we've listed these steps as a simple sequence. But they don't always appear that way. One of the moves may only be implied, may be made more than once, or moves may overlap. Introductions to short papers are more likely to make the four moves in a clear sequence. In longer papers, authors often use this variation: Make the first three or all four moves briefly first—then back up and cover moves 2 and 3 in greater detail. This lets readers quickly see what your research offers. If they are interested, they will then take the time to read your more detailed discussion of prior research and how your new work fits into it. In fact, we're going to tell you to describe these same things again but in more detail in the Literature Review/Theory section. This may seem redundant, but it makes the paper more useful for a variety of readers—those who are already familiar with theory and the area of research and those who are not. This form also resulted from scientists' need to scan many more research papers than they have time to read carefully. Often we just read the abstract or the introduction and then skip straight to the tables and figures.

Working with sources is not just an important part of writing Introductions—it's the main stuff of moves 1–3. Here are examples from different papers showing how sources are commonly used in the first three moves.

Move 1: Announce the Topic and Explain Its Importance

Provide background information:

In 1997, government funding accounted for 37 percent of the nonprofit sector's revenue, up from 31 percent in 1977 (**Salamon 2002**).

In 1980, women caught up to men in their voting rates and have surpassed them in every subsequent election (**US Bureau of the Census 2006**).

Many of the basic risk factors for adolescent suicidality are well known; among these, the most important are depression [**2,4–6**], exposure to suicide or suicide attempts by family or friends [**7,8**], substance or alcohol abuse [**9**], and having guns in the home [**2,10,11**].

Move 2: Give an Overview of Prior Research

Summarize prior research:

Similarly, **ethnographic evidence shows** that charitable acts and volunteering are common when they are embedded in the social structure of a community **(Eckstein 2001)**.

Muslims are also diverse with respect to factors that are central to contemporary theories of US political incorporation, namely, religious identity (secular and devout), social class (ranging from professional to working class), nativity, and generational status **(for a review, see Leighley and Vedlitz 1999)**.

Quote from prior research:

Frumkin (2002) notes that "[w]hile volunteers remain an important engine driving nonprofits, most nonprofits use professionals to manage volunteers, rather than using volunteers to manage their organizations" **(p. 102)**.

In their study of several dozen San Francisco nonprofits, Kramer and Grossman (1987) **observed that** it was "exceedingly difficult [for government] not to renew a contract if the provider . . . can mobilize community support" (p. 43).

Move 3: Establish the Gap

Refer to multiple studies, noting the different limitations of each:

Evans, Orians, and Ascher (1992) tried to estimate the number of potential donors but did not analyze procurement data. **Siminoffand Nelson (1999)** studied the efficiency of OPOs but confined themselves to a particular UNOS region. **A study by Ozcan, Begun, and McKinney (1999)** focused on organizational measures of efficiency but did not control for any structural variables.

Refer to multiple studies, addressing the same limitation for all:

However, less attention has been paid to gender differences in the foundations of such differences . . . and the dearth is particularly evident in research on immigrant political incorporation, where the overwhelming majority of work has focused on men's experiences **(Gerstle and Mollenkopf 2001; Portes and Rumbaut 2001).**

Refer to multiple studies showing conflicting findings:

However, the evidence on how religious identity affects political participation **is mixed. Some find that** Islamic beliefs discourage participation in US politics **(Khan 2003), whereas others find that** religious involvement is positively associated with political participation for Arab Muslims but less so for South-Asian and African American Muslims **(Jamal 2005b).** A lack of quality measures on religious identity contributes to these mixed findings . . .

Move 4: Explain How Your Research Helps Fill the Gap

Unlike moves 1–3, move 4 is often made without citations. In the following examples, we begin with the end of move 3. Notice how first-person pronouns signal the shift to move 4. (Using "I" or "we" is acceptable in scientific writing. For a discussion of how and when to use it, see pp. 201–206.) Here's the first example:

However, these studies often fail to address the critical questions of how, when, and for whom does suggestion matter? **With this study, we** employ three waves of data from the National Longitudinal Study of Adolescent Health to examine these questions. **By using** longitudinal data rich in measures of adolescent life, <u>**we**</u> **investigate** the role suicide suggestion plays in the suicide process, independent of other measures of social integration and psychological well-being. <u>**We**</u> **tease out** nuances related to the harmful side of social integration by shedding light on four major gaps in the literature: (1) whether suicide suggestion is associated with the development of suicidal thoughts among individuals who reported no suicidal thoughts at the time a role model attempted suicide; (2) whether the effects of suicide suggestion fade with time; (3) whether . . .

Here's another example:

This work, however, often draws on small, nonrepresentative samples **and focuses specifically on** the narratives of those struggling with name-change decisions or on perceptions of name changers and keepers. **In addition, most research has not explored** Americans' general attitudes about the longstanding tradition.

   In this article <u>**we**</u> **take the next step, looking at** Americans' views on name change as one possible indicator of gender attitudes, more broadly conceived. <u>**We**</u> **contend that there is a need to revisit our approach to** gender attitude assessment as the presence of women in the workplace—long the primary topic for survey research on gender beliefs—has become commonplace, even expected. <u>**We**</u> **present** marital name change **as one potential avenue into** contemporary gender attitudes, using it primarily to illustrate . . .

A common variation on moves 3 and 4 is to establish the gap (move 3) by presenting two or more competing views on a sociological question and then (move 4) stating that your intention is to test the competing claims through new research:

> The salience of athletics in adolescent culture fuels ongoing debates about the social role of youth sports. **On the one hand, proponents have long argued that** interscholastic athletics positively impact adolescent development...
>
> **Critical scholars, however, assail traditional views of** youth sports **as incomplete and problematic. . . . Rather than** building socially competent young men and women, **it is suggested,** the conditions of contemporary athletics embed youth in value systems marred by homophobia, sexism, racism, and ruthless competition. . . . **Rejecting the view that** sports help to curb antisocial behavior, **some researchers assert that** the hypermasculine cultures characteristic of many contact sports teach violence as an acceptable means of maintaining valued male identities...
>
> **Answering this question has important implications for** school-based sporting programs, **yet surprisingly little research has addressed** the youth sports–violence relationship. **Moreover, studies that have been conducted generally suffer from methodological limitations...**
>
> **In this article, I move beyond prior research** with theoretically grounded hypotheses and advanced quantitative methods. **I rely on three distinct theoretical traditions**—social control, social learning, and masculinity theories—**to derive competing hypotheses for** the sports–violence relationship. **I then test these for** five

very different sports—football, basketball, baseball, wrestling, and tennis—using data from . . .

No matter which variations of these moves you use, you want to get to move 4 fairly quickly. Remember that your Introduction is only that: an introduction to your work. Resist the impulse to tell your reader too much at this stage. The Intro should read more like a roadmap than a travelogue.

CHECKLIST FOR WRITING INTRODUCTIONS

Does your introduction . . .

✓ Clearly introduce the topic? The Introduction should begin by introducing the topic briefly yet clearly enough that readers unfamiliar with it can understand the general area of this research.

✓ Clearly outline prior research? The Introduction should provide a quick but useful and coherent overview of prior research. (Think of it as an outline to the literature review in the next section, discussing only those key sources needed to establish the research "gap.")

✓ Clearly establish the research gap? The Introduction should clearly establish the hole in knowledge that the present work is intended to help fill.

✓ Clearly explain how the present work contributes to filling the gap? The Introduction should state the *kind(s)* of evidence you have collected and explain *how* that evidence helps fill the gap. (In other words, what we know from your research that we didn't know before.)

✓ Clearly signal which move is occurring at each point? The moves only work if your readers can tell *which* moves you are making!

Reviewing the Literature

Unlike natural scientists, sociologists use an exceptionally wide range of methods and theories. As a result, they cannot assume that even expert readers will be familiar with the prior research or the key concepts and terms they will use. So before beginning to discuss their research, they often need to explain the relevant theories, concepts, and terms and discuss how these are relevant for their study. In the shortest papers, this background information might be integrated into the Introduction—typically in moves 2, 3 and/or 4. Long papers usually have a separate Literature Review and Theory sections (or one of each) between the Introduction and Methods. These sections are usually longer than the Introduction and are often divided into subsections with separate headings.

The purpose of the Theory and Literature Review section is to situate your research project within sociological theory and prior research. You'll need to identify the literature that is most important for readers of your paper—both theoretical and empirical. Then you'll present that body of literature in a way that (1) explains/defines key concepts and terms, (2) summarizes the relevant (for your research) knowledge contained in that literature, and (3) shows where there is consensus and

Tips for Your Literature Review

- Don't assume your readers are familiar with the reports or theories to which you're referring. Consider which terms will you need to define or explain.
- Don't organize the references by date or—even worse—the order in which you found them. Organize them as they relate to what you are doing in *your* research.

where there is substantive disagreement among the sources or a missing element that represents a gap in knowledge.

Some papers combine theoretical and empirical (evidence-based) articles into one section. Others break them out into two separate sections. Your decision (if your professor doesn't give you a format to follow) will depend on the type of research question you ask and the literature that is relevant to it. We'll explain.

Sometimes the entire literature about a question is centered around a single theory that defines the concepts and guides the questions that are studied. In that case, it would make more sense to describe the theory first, defining its concepts, and then to talk about the empirical studies that lead to the specific question you want to ask. Other times there are sets of studies that describe a pattern (like who marries whom) that can be understood through the lens of a particular theory (like exchange theory). In that case, you might want to describe the empirical papers first, and then introduce the theory that you think best explains them. Or there might be two different theoretical schools that are both talking about the same thing. (This theory competition is rarer than you might think: Usually a theory defines what is important to study, and it's unusual for two *different* theories to define things exactly the same way). In that case, you might describe the two different theoretical/research literatures, before coming to your study that can help decide between them for some particular situation. Here's the bottom line in deciding whether to discuss the theory or empirical references first: start with whichever defines your research question.

It can be confusing to sort out what goes in the Introduction and what goes in the Literature Review. Think of the Introduction as an outline of your Literature Review and Theory, and the Literature Review/Theory sections as the fleshed-out version of the Introduction. But even in the "fleshed-out" version, you still need to be selective. You won't discuss each source as extensively as you would for the book review or article description assignments that we discussed in Chapter 2 (p. 16–19). Just focus on what your reader needs to know about a source to further your argument. Try to get someone (or even your computer) to read your Literature Review and Theory section to you. It should be understandable in audible form—telling a story of what we know, where the gaps are, and what we can build on to fill them.

Here are examples of moves that you might make in a Literature Review/Theory section:

Applying a theory or model

[**T**]he aging-as-leveler **hypothesis posits that** aging involves negative consequences for both advantaged and disadvantaged populations, and that those with advantages earlier in life have the most to lose in later life (**Dowd and Bengtson 1978**). This hypothesis predicts that . . .

The group identity **model is especially relevant for** Muslim Americans, **given** the growing research that links religious group identity to political participation among other minorities, such as African Americans (**Harris 1994, 1999; Patillo-McCoy 1998**).

Summarizing to define key terms

For this study **we rely on the definition of** salience **developed by Stryker's (1991)** identity theory. **According to this** conceptualization, salience **is the** likelihood that an individual will act in accord with certain expectations across various situations.

Quoting to define key terms

In everyday usage, an altruistic act is one motivated by concern or regard for others rather than oneself. **Simmons (1991) gives a useful definition**: "Although scholars' definitions differ, most would agree that altruism (1) seeks to increase another's welfare, not one's own; (2) is voluntary; (3) is intentional, meant to help someone else; and (4) expects no external reward" (p. 3). **According to Sober and Wilson (1998)**, "The altruism hypothesis maintains that people sometimes care about the welfare of others as an end in itself. Altruists have irreducible other-directed ends" (p. 228).

Tip: Beware of the Sequential Presentation of Sources!

A common mistake students make in writing a literature review is discussing their sources sequentially. This amounts to "Here's what's in source 1, here's what's in source 2, . . . " The document ends up reading like a series of dull, high-school-style book reports. Novices sometimes do this by default (it seems logical enough) and sometimes out of deference for established researchers (who am I to speak back to the experts?). Experienced academic writers, however, organize their literature reviews by putting their sources into conversation.

A clue that you're going about this in the wrong way is if you have a separate paragraph for each source. Instead, most of your paragraphs should begin with a point *you* want to make—a statement about an issue, question, or

continued

continued
claim, and then proceed to discuss the relevant sources in relation to that point. That's the synthesis your readers need. For longer papers, some writers use headings and subheadings to announce topics and then cluster relevant sources under the heading.

In addition, you may need to reference some of your sources more than once in your literature review section, since important sources will often be relevant for more than one issue you want to discuss related to your research question.

While you will most likely want to avoid discussing your sources sequentially, there are exceptions: Sometimes a very coherent theoretical literature will build systematically from each piece of evidence to the next question. In that case, your literature review will be close to sequential. But that's just because the development of the literature is so driven by the theory and so tightly interrelated.

Writing Your Hypothesis

Literature review/theory sections often end with a set of hypotheses. This is more common with quantitative papers than with qualitative ones, because qualitative work is more likely to explore an understudied group or to inductively develop theory. If you do present hypotheses at the end of this section (or perhaps one at the end of each subsection that develops the ideas that lead up to it), there are some things to keep in mind.

Be sure to number each hypothesis.
This will allow you to refer back to it easily when you are writing your Results section.

Make sure that each hypothesis relates to just *one* pattern of findings.

You want your answer for each hypothesis to be "supported" or "not supported." Having more than one prediction in a single hypothesis could lead to "well, yes and no" as your answer—and that's confusing. For example, a good hypothesis might be:

Hypothesis 1: Having a child will increase the probability of parental obesity after the birth.

In contrast, the following complex hypothesis would be better if broken into three separate predictions:

Not this: Getting married and having children will increase the probability of parental obesity.

But this:

Hypothesis 1: Getting married will increase the probability of parental obesity.

Hypothesis 2: Having a first child will increase the probability of parental obesity.

Hypothesis 3: Each additional birth will increase the probability of parental obesity.

Notice that even these hypotheses are a bit complex, in the sense that marriage and childbirth might affect men and women differently. There, at least, you could describe your results as supporting H1 for men but not for women, and so on. However, if you had reasons to *predict* different patterns for men and women, you'd want to state that explicitly in your hypotheses. All of this expansion means that you might end up with a lot of hypotheses. That's okay because it makes your predictions clear and will make writing up your results much easier.

Sometimes the concrete variables that you will use to measure your concepts aren't presented until your Methods section. In that case, you might first describe these in a Theoretical Propositions subsection of your Literature Review and Theory section; you can then elaborate on these in a Hypotheses subsection in your Methods section—after you present your measurement of those concepts in your data. For example:

> Proposition 1: Organization size will be positively correlated with organization differentiation.

Might become:

> Hypothesis 1: The number of members will be positively correlated with the number of committees of campus organizations.

CHECKLIST FOR WRITING THEORY/LITERATURE REVIEW SECTIONS

✓ **Do you begin by establishing a theoretical frame?** An effective Literature Review/Theory section often begins by establishing a theoretical foundation for the research. What is the major theoretical work on which this research is developed? How is your research question connected to the theory?

✓ **Is the selection of sources appropriate?** An effective Literature Review/Theory section will review a carefully selected body of the most relevant prior research, including only references that help readers understand your research.

✓ **Is the section well organized?** The Literature Review/Theory section should identify a small number of key questions raised in the literature important to your research; the discussion should be structured around those questions. Most paragraphs should begin with statements that present (or continue discussion of) one of these questions and proceed to discuss each of the sources relevant for that question in relation to one another.

✓ **Does the section have an effective conclusion?** Readers will want you to help them understand what this literature means for the research they are about to read. So at the end of the section, present a clearly articulated set of questions that your research addresses. You may choose to follow this with stated hypotheses for what you expected to find from your research. Remember that those hypotheses should come from prior research or the theories that you are working with; they aren't just hunches pulled out of thin air. If you have them, review your hypotheses to make sure that they are not double-barreled. They should allow for only binary 'yes or 'no' answers.

Writing Methods

The Methods section of a research report has two purposes—one practical, one rhetorical. The practical one is to explain what you did clearly enough that readers could replicate your study to verify your findings—if they wanted to. In reality, few studies get duplicated in this way, so the second purpose is the more important: to make an argument that you conducted your research in a way that readers (especially your professor) will judge to be appropriate for your research question and adequate to support the claims that you make about your findings.

We suggest that you write at least part of your Methods section right after you finish writing a draft of your Introduction. If you think of the first draft of your Introduction as a memo to yourself and your professor about the aims of your research and how it ties in with the existing literature, the first draft of your Methods will be a memo explaining how you plan to acquire your evidence.

Just as for the Introduction, there will be some things you'll need to include in your final Methods section that you won't yet know—like how many interviews you'll have time to conduct or exactly which variables you will use. But if you put the decisions that you *can* make up front on paper (like the description of the database and your core variables, or the questions that you will ask in your in-depth interviews and how you will find people to interview), you'll be forced to think concretely about how to proceed with your research. It may seem scary to make those decisions, but putting them off just delays the process and makes you more rushed later. Your best option is to start with a rough 'sketch'—an overview of the general approach you plan to use—and get feedback on that. Then use that feedback to revise your plan and write a more complete draft of Methods.

Because sociology encompasses a wide range of methodologies, each with its own set of expectations and norms, we can provide only general tips for writing methods—not detailed guidance. For the latter, we recommend that you find examples of published research using methods similar to your own work and model your writing after those. Don't worry about the topic—it's only the research process that needs to be similar. If you can find a suitable model that divides the section into labeled subsections, that will give you the clearest guide for what you might include. Now, here are those tips, with some examples.

Describing Databases

If you used data collected by others:

- Give the official name of the database.
- Cite it well enough that someone else could locate the data source.

- Describe the sample and data collection process briefly—enough so readers can get a sense of the data, expecting that if they want more information they'll go to your cited sources.

Many databases, especially the major ones like ICPSR (Inter-University Consortium for Political and Social Research), will tell you how to cite them. For others, you can often locate the first publication using the database that describes it in detail. That's a good source to cite. Citing where you downloaded it from is useful, too. For example, here is the description of the database from the study of social media influence on drinking discussed earlier:

Data were drawn from the **Social Network Study**, a longitudinal study of high school adolescents designed to answer methodological and theoretical questions about data collection practices and effects of different peer relationships on risk outcomes [34]. The sample consisted of 10th-grade students at five comprehensive high schools in the El Monte Union High School District. (These five high schools comprised the entire school district. None of these schools are considered charter or magnet schools.)

database name

what it is

citation

description

Describing Your Own Data Collection

If you are collecting your own data, explain how you selected participants for your study and what kind of data you collected from them. If you studied something other than people (organizations or countries or advertisements), explain how you decided if a unit was eligible for your study and whether you studied that entire population or sampled from it. If you did any coding or variable development, explain that, too. Here's a student example of qualitative research showing some typical moves:

Interviews

This study draws on in-depth, semistructured interviews with 31 juniors and seniors at an elite, private university in New England. Over the course of four and a half months, I conducted 5 pilot interviews and 31 interviews with juniors and seniors.

Because no randomized research pool or list was available at the university, participants were recruited through snowball sampling. In an effort to interview respondents from all walks of campus life, I did not start by interviewing anyone I knew directly. I made initial contact with prospective respondents by email. No compensation was offered in return for participation. In total, my response rate was about 60 percent.

I conducted all interviews personally in private offices and study rooms from November 10, 2012, to February 22, 2013. With respondents' consent, all interviews were digitally recorded and transcribed verbatim. Interview length ranged from a minimum of 1 hour to a maximum of 2 hours and 45 minutes, with an average of about 110 minutes.

I began every interview by informing the respondent that the general topic of the interview was "love" and offering the first task as a simple word association for the word "love." General questions included: "Have you ever been in a romantic relationship?" "How do you express love?" Probes included: "When you said 'I love you,' what did that mean?" "How do you think your love relationships will be different as you get older?"

Uses subheads

Briefly: Who was studied and how?

How were participants recruited?

Conditions for participation?

Response rate

Setting of data collection

What questions did you ask? What information did you collect?

> ### Analysis
> Using grounded theory methodology, I transcribed and coded the interviews as I went along using Atlas.ti 7.1, refining and adding questions to my interview guide as needed for a final total of 17 core questions. I derived codes by substantive and selective coding, reading each transcript multiple times and writing memos to draw out general themes and narrow my focus. I began writing my final analysis after conducting, transcribing, and coding all 31 interviews.

How did you process and analyze the data?

Even though quantitative studies are very different in design, many of the moves for describing methods are similar. Here are excerpts from a student paper that actually got published showing the beginning of each subsection:

Participants and Setting

I conducted this study using Amazon Mechanical Turk (MTurk), a crowdsourcing website which has been increasingly adopted by social scientists as a venue for recruiting participants. The site allows researchers to ...

Study Narrative Description and Experimental Conditions

The protagonist of this study's narrative is Eric, a 28-year-old textile mill worker faced with losing his job. He is described as ...

Procedure

Participants were told that they would be given 10 minutes to read though the story twice, and would be

continued

expected to reproduce it later in the experiment to be read by the next participant in their chain. They were prompted to imagine . . . Once the 10 minutes had elapsed, participants were redirected to a distractor . . .

Key Outcome Variables and Narrative Coding Process

The primary outcome variables in this study are counts of total, stereotype-consistent, and stereotype-inconsistent statements maintained, added, and transmitted (#maintained + #added) in participant reproduced narratives. To measure these changes, each statement of each participant's reproduced narrative was coded into one of five categories—maintained, lost . . .

Coding proceeded in two stages. In the first, each participant's narrative was coded . . .

Analytical Strategy

Data were analyzed using a multilevel Poisson model with . . .

Of course, some studies don't directly study people. Here's an example of a study that coded tweets to study Occupy Wall Street. Again, note how the subheads clearly indicate the author's purpose for each part:

Selection of Cases

To empirically explore the impact of Twitter on social and political actions, we selected three highly visible movements that mobilized in 2011 and 2012:

the *indignados* (known also as the 15M movement) in Spain, the *aganaktismenoi* in Greece, and OWS in the United States. These three movements are chosen because they were directly influenced by, and identified with, the "true democracy" aims of the Arab Spring mobilizations, but also because they were in direct dialogue and solidarity with each other. (The authors then go on to further discuss why these movements are particularly good for a Twitter study.)

Data Collection and Sampling
To assess whether the three movements used Twitter in a similar fashion, tweets were collected using the social media crawler and text analytic tool *Discovertext* for two weeks during the heydays of protest in each country (June 5–19, 2011, for Spain and Greece; October 2–16, 2011, for the US protests). The results presented here are based on content analysis of a random sample of 2000 tweets drawn from each movement using the #15M (80,074 tweets), #greekrevolution (19,784 tweets), and #occupywallstreet (342,479 tweets).

Defining Categories
After drawing the sample, two of the authors initially separately scanned the content of 60 tweets from the Greek and Spanish data sets (30 for each case) for the purpose of listing the distinct categories which could reveal how Twitter was used for political action. After discussing the results, the procedure was repeated three times, examining in total 90 tweets each for each country data set.

continued

Coding and Intercoder Reliability Tests
After reaching acceptable levels of intercoder reliability in each of the categories, three research assistants (Spanish-, Greek-, and English-speaking) were recruited for the coding, and the three collections of tweets were loaded into custom-made software (see supplementary material). [The authors then go on to describe the software and the reliability tests.]

Method of Analysis
Classic social network analysis measures such as in- and out-degree centrality to define the position and influence of certain actors within the networks are applied. We analyzed the information automatically retrieved from Twitter, such as whether the tweet includes a link, whether it is original or retweeted, and whether it is directed to a specific user.

CHECKLIST FOR WRITING METHODS

✓ *Does the section contain only methods material?* The section should not include, for example, results or interpretation of results.

✓ *Do you include sufficient but not excessive detail?* Although you cannot include every possible detail of your study, you should include enough so readers will clearly understand what you did. Should they wish to verify your results, they should have enough information to do a reasonable replication of your study.

✓ *Is the section well organized?* Methods should be presented in subsections covering the major dimensions of your methods, organized according to the conventions of the subfield of your project. An in-depth interview study will have different headings than an analysis of secondary survey data. Material in each section should be presented in a logical order.

Writing a Research Proposal

Because research requires money, sociology professors often write research proposals to convince funding organizations to support research they want to do. Graduate students sometimes write them as well—to support their thesis or dissertation work or to fund summer research. Some schools have similar programs for undergraduate research. If you're interested in getting funding for an undergraduate research project, try searching your school's website for "undergraduate research" or just contacting an academic dean.

Professors often assign research proposals as a course assignment when they want students to get experience thinking and writing about research but know that students won't have the time or expertise needed to complete a full research project. These proposals give students practice in locating a literature, formulating a research question based on a gap in that literature, and devising a data collection strategy and analysis plan that could answer the question.

The research proposal (sometimes called a "grant proposal" or just a "grant" if it's actually being submitted for funding) shares many parts and features of the research report. If you think of the proposal as a research report without the Results and Discussion sections, you'll be pretty close. (Although it's unlikely you'll be asked to include it, proposals sometimes require something similar to the Discussion section of a research report called Anticipated Results that explains what you expect to find and what that would mean.) The biggest difference between the proposal and the report is that the proposal describes research you *propose to do*, rather than what you've done. At its core, the proposal is an argument that a research question is worth investigating and that you have a good way to study it. A professional proposal might actually include *more* detail than a report about the importance of the study and the methods because those are the things that will show most clearly whether or not your project is worth doing—and therefore worth funding. Like everything else connected to research, a good sociological research question is essential.

What Is a Good Proposal?

Writing an effective proposal requires that you understand your audience. For the typical social science research proposal, that audience is more tightly defined than for many kinds of writing. Unless you are told otherwise, assume that your readers:

- are knowledgeable about the field of sociology generally,
- are *not* experts in the subfield of your research, and
- *do not* have prior knowledge of your research topic.

A successful proposal will convince such readers that your research will help address a meaningful gap in knowledge and that your methods for doing this are appropriate and practical. Be specific about what you plan to do. The best proposals are clear enough that someone else could carry out your research project successfully without you there to guide them. This means including specifics such as actual measures, survey questions, or an interview guide.

Which Details to Include

How much detail you include in a research proposal will depend a lot on the assignment (or, in the real world, directions from the potential funding agency). A proposal for summer research at your school might be only a few pages long. Full-blown proposals can be as long as full research reports: 10 or 20 pages. The space that would have been taken up by results and discussion is given over to more detail on methods, data, analysis plans, and an explanation of the significance of the research. If you are writing a real grant proposal rather than just a class assignment, you would also include these items:

- a time line for accomplishing different tasks in the project, to give the reviewers a clear sense that you know what the steps will be and that they can be accomplished in a reasonable amount of time
- a budget

Want to Get Funded? Follow the Rules!

If you are writing a proposal in hopes of actually funding a research project, treat the grant report guidelines as gospel. Requirements for things like page or word limits, major sections, what should be included and so on aren't just suggestions. Reviewers typically receive many more viable proposals than they have funds to support, and they'll take any excuse to put a proposal in the "reject" pile and concentrate on the others. So get the details right! Before submitting a proposal, read through the Call for Proposals (CFP) carefully and highlight each required component in a copy of your paper to make sure you didn't miss something. Then read it again regularly as you draft and revise you proposal.

Getting IRB Approval

If you are doing a real research project and plan to make your findings public, you may need to get approval for your research from your school's institutional review board (IRB). IRB approval is the process that your institution uses to protect human participants in any research. This process is complex, important, and varies a great deal by institution. We can only give you a few basics here. The folks who work at the IRB office can assist you in figuring out whether you need approval and, if so, how to go about getting it. Don't hesitate to ask for their help.

Basically, you need to get IRB approval if you are doing research that involves collecting any kind of data on human or: animal subjects. *Research* has a specific meaning in the IRB: it means that you are trying to contribute to a scientific literature and might present your results at a professional meeting or publish them. The kind of pseudo-research projects often assigned in classes just for educational purposes don't usually require IRB approval—although your professor might want you to go through the process so that you understand it. To get approval to do your research as a student, your professor or some other employee of the institution will have to supervise your work and sign your IRB protocol. Because your school is certifying that your research will be conducted according to established ethical standards, they want an experienced professional within their system to have ultimate responsibility.

An IRB protocol has very specific parts; your school will have a website that will describe exactly what is needed. You'll be asked to provide a description of how you will select participants, how you will interact with them, what information you will collect from them, and what you will do with that information. You'll need to give a short explanation of the scientific background for the project (about the same amount as in the Introduction to a research report but in less technical language), so the IRB folks can balance any potential risk to subjects against the scientific value of the study. Most of the content of the IRB protocol is focused on methods, though. You will need to be much more specific here than you are in your actual research report. Going through the IRB process is valuable—not only because it protects your participants from possible harm but it also gets you to make all of those really hard decisions about who you will study, how you'll find them, and what you will do.

Getting an IRB protocol approved takes time—often a month or more. Therefore, find out at the very beginning of your project whether or not you'll need IRB approval for your project. If you do, you can't collect *any* data until after your proposed procedures have been approved. Once you get approval, you need to do things exactly they way you said you would do. If you change anything about your project (including seemingly minor things like how many interviews you do and how your message to potential participants is worded), you need to file an "amendment" to your IRB protocol—with your professor's signature. Fortunately, amendments typically take much less time to get reviewed. This process may seem cumbersome, but your professors have to go through it every time they collect new evidence from human participants. Reading some of the truly horrendous stories of what people have done to others in the past in the name of science makes you understand that the protection of human subjects is well worth the extra work.

As you might have guessed, you can usually avoid the IRB process altogether by using databases rather than collecting your own data—so that's another advantage of going this route. The people who collected those data and made it publicly available have already been through the IRB process, assuring that their participants were protected appropriately. Be sure to check, however; some schools want you to fill out a simple form so that they can check to make sure that the database is, in fact, legitimate and thus followed proper protocol.

6

WRITING ABOUT YOUR ORIGINAL RESEARCH: *AFTER* YOU HAVE DATA

If you've followed our advice to this point and already written drafts of your Introduction and Methods sections, take 10 minutes for yourself. Sit quietly and relax, do some yoga, or watch a YouTube video of cats playing the piano. You've earned it.

OK, Time's up. Now that you've collected your evidence, it's time to start writing your Results and Discussion sections. Once you've drafted these sections, you'll need to revise the Introduction and Methods sections to make sure they match what you actually did, as well as set the reader up for your conclusions.

Writing About Your Results

Scientists often use the expression "writing up the results." For the novice, this can be misleading in two ways: First, it makes it seem as if the experts go straight from collecting data to writing a finished version of the Results section. But perhaps more than anywhere else in the research report, *writing* is *where the thinking happens*. As you write down what you've found, you begin to see the patterns in your data. Second, composing your results isn't merely writing prose. If you've done any quantitative work, a major part of this writing is constructing the tables, graphs, and charts that let you—and eventually your reader—see the patterns that matter. If you collected qualitative data, you might construct visual representations of those data, too.

As you can tell, the ways in which you eventually present your results will depend on the kind of data you collect. If you are using quantitative methods, you will need to develop the skills of statistical analysis and designing tables, charts, and graphs. If you are using qualitative methods such as interviews or ethnography, you will learn how to write with quotations and do "thick description."

Each kind of evidence has its own conventions and requirements. For example, quantitative researchers often begin the Results section with a table giving basic descriptive statistics for each of the major variables: the mean/mode/median, the range of responses, the variance, and so on. Obviously, that

"A common mistake that qualitative researchers make is they feel it is necessary to include every piece of relevant research data in their writing. This can lead to a kind of 'ice cream cone' version of research writing, where quotations and descriptions are heaped upon each other without purpose. . . . Often less data can be more effecting or persuasive as long as it captures vividly the point the writer is trying to make."

—Les Back, "Take Your Reader There: Some Notes on Writing Qualitative Research" [https://www.dur.ac.uk/writingacrossboundaries/writingonwriting/lesback/]

convention doesn't apply to qualitative research. To communicate your findings effectively, you will need to learn some of these conventions. Look for a few good models to guide you.

But perhaps the most important principle in presenting results applies to all types of data: Don't expect the data to speak for themselves! Whether it's a table, a graph, or a quotation, the most common way that novices miss the mark is by assuming that if they *show*, they don't need to *tell*. In fact, professionals can miss this mark, too: One of us reviewed a paper for publication that had six figures, each with three panels. The description of these 18 visuals was only three short paragraphs. Even an expert reviewer couldn't figure out what one was supposed to see in those figures. So we will explain how to do both parts of the task: choosing which data to present and describing those data in ways that let your readers understand what's important to see.

The Structure of Results Sections

Results sections of some published sociology research reports may run 10 pages or more. Given the limited amount of time (and thus data) available for class research projects, you'll probably be expected to write only a few pages of results. But don't let length scare you; most of the Results section is built up from a number of smaller units, each built around a *statement of finding* in which the authors explain or suggest a meaning for a specific research result.[1] Although there are many different kinds of such statements in sociology research, here are three common categories with examples of each:

Comparison: Showing whether data for some measure differ between two or more subsets of the sample.

---

[1] This discussion draws on Brett, Paul. "The Results Section in Sociology Articles." *English for Specific Purposes* 13(1): 47–59, 1994.

Parental divorce approximately doubled the odds that off-spring would see their own marriages end in divorce. Off-spring with maritally distressed parents who remained continuously married did not have an elevated risk of divorce.

Time-related change: Showing whether data change (or don't) over a period of time.

Results from unconditional growth curve models with no covariates indicate that, on average, body weight increases over time (b = 0.061; $p < .001$) for the 3,617 individuals included in the analyses.

Association: Showing whether a change in one variable correlates with a change in another.

Table 2 compares parents to childless individuals; these results indicate that, net of controls, parents and nonparents began the study period with similar weight levels (latent intercept, indicating baseline body weight) but that, compared to the childless, parents experienced more rapid weight gain (latent slope, indicating the rate of change in body weight over time) over the 15-year study period (b = 0.046, $p < .01$).

A fourth type we might call the "ditto statement." This is a shortcut stating that what you just said about some other variables, groups, and so forth applies to these others as well:

Results in Table 3 show no significant main effects of any of the parenting transitions on weight change between time points, net of controls. [Here's the ditto:] We also assessed possible interactions of parenting transitions with gender. Only four of 54 interaction terms attained statistical significance and yielded no consistent pattern of results.

Now that you have a sense of the objective of these findings statements, let's look at how they are typically constructed. A findings paragraph (or group of paragraphs) typically begins with a *pointer* statement indicating which data are going to be discussed. This might be a reference to a graph or table, to a mathematical model, or just to the variables under consideration.

Table 4 shows the estimated treatment effects of mission trips on matched groups, using nearest-neighbor matching . . . **The analyses reveal** that the effect of mission trip is statistically significant for a variety of outcomes related to <u>religious beliefs</u> and <u>practices</u> . . .

Pointer for unit

Intro to unit: specifying two subunits: (a) *beliefs* and (b) *practices*

Compared to professing a <u>belief</u> in God, individuals who went on a mission trip **are significantly less likely to** report that they are unsure about their belief in God. Going on a mission trip also **decreases the likelihood** of viewing God as an impersonal force and increases feelings of closeness to God. Adolescents who went on a mission trip between waves **are more likely to** agree that it is OK to convert others; however, mission trips **neither increase nor decrease** religious doubt among those who go relative to those who do not . . .

Statements of findings: (a)

Going on a mission trip also **results in increased** <u>religiosity</u> along several different dimensions of religious practice. Mission trips **predict increases in** attendance at

Statements of findings: (b)

religious services and private Bible reading and prayer, **as well as an increased likelihood of** actually proselytizing individuals of a different faith.

In short, mission trips intensify traditional and orthodox religious <u>beliefs</u> among the adolescents who participate in them, but they fail to buffer against the experience of religious doubt. Mission trips also increase religious <u>practice</u> along all of the dimensions examined here.

Summary statements for unit

Words as Data: Summarizing, Paraphrasing, and Quoting

Qualitative methods offer a different view into sociological issues than do quantitative approaches. Qualitative findings allow us to better understand how groups of people see some aspect of their lives. Whereas quantitative researchers describe the relationship between variables or test theoretical ideas, qualitative researchers are often trying to develop new concepts or theoretical understandings that can be used in future research. If you are collecting qualitative

> "Qualitative methods express the assumptions... that there are multiple realities that are socially defined. Rich description persuades by showing that the researcher was immersed in the setting and giving the reader enough detail to 'make sense' of the situation."
>
> —William Firestone, *Meaning in Method: The Rhetoric of Quantitative and Qualitative Research*

data, you may focus on experiences that your research participants had or the language that they use to describe themselves or others. Whether your research involves surveys, interviews, observations, or conversations, much of your data will be verbal.

There are three common ways for sharing specific verbal data with readers: summary, description, and quotation. When you review the data you collected, what *patterns* do you see? These patterns are findings you want to summarize. Typically, when you summarize a finding, you'll want to follow up with one or more descriptions or quotations as examples to show your readers precisely what you mean. Such examples serve not so much as sufficient evidence but as a means to help your readers better understand the situations or experiences you are discussing. Here are the three again:

- *Summarize:* State a trend or finding from your data.
- *Describe:* Share examples from your data that illustrate your finding or provide particular cases (individuals) that help readers better imagine the people and places you encountered.
- *Quote:* Show your readers what your subjects *themselves* said in relation to the trend you are discussing.

In the passage that follows, the authors begin with a summary statement of a general finding. This is followed by a described example and then a case that combines description and quotation.

Although quotations and visuals offer very different kinds of evidence, some of the principles underlying effective use are the same: Be explicit about the point you want to make with the evidence and then point to the specific features that support that general point. In other words, guide your reader in interpreting the evidence. Just like a graph, every quotation

---

[M]others in the study often neglected their own physical and mental health needs to meet the economic and health care needs of their children and other family members. . . . **For example, some mothers** refused to take medication prescribed for hypertension because they feared it would keep them from being "alert enough" to care for their young children. **Rena, for instance,** sleeping only 5 hours a night, was too busy and too worried about the impact of medications to follow medical advice.

A 25-year-old single mother of three children aged 1, 5, and 10, she worked the third shift . . . Diagnosed with clinical depression and absorbed as she was in the care for her 10-year-old autistic child and her two younger children with asthma, Rena had "little time to be depressed."

> State finding
>
> Description of *specific* trend observed in data that supports the finding
>
> Presentation of case as example of the trend

---

offers a number of possible meanings and it's up to you to show your reader what's important for *your* analysis. Another good practice for both kinds of evidence is to include only those data that are relevant; for quotations, this means selecting the fewest number of words needed to fairly represent the source and to make your point. Anything more only serves to distract your reader from the words that are important to you. In our example, note how the author's quotation from Rena includes only five of Rena's actual words.

Let's look some more at quotation length by noticing the different choices the author makes in the following example. The first quotation contains three complete sentences; this long excerpt is best presented as a block quotation. The three remaining quotes in this paragraph are *in-line* quotations. Only one of these is in complete sentences; the other two are trimmed down to just a few words that get the point across.

Another way to present interview data is in dialogue form. This is a good choice if the exchange between interviewer and interviewee is interesting and the responses are brief:

For example, one common way respondents explained why it was better for women to change their names was to identify collectivist sources that dictate the practice— namely, religion, tradition, and/or society. Some of the most vocal name-change advocates turned to the Bible (although name change became practice well after the biblical era). **Their responses suggest that women must follow religiously proscribed gender practices—despite their own feelings on the issue.** One respondent noted,

State your point or claim.

Give *your* interpretation of quotations.

> Woman was made out of man, and therefore man is the head of the house. I know the feminine isn't gonna like that, but that's the way the biblical standard is. That doesn't mean the woman is a slave to anybody or anything else, but it does mean just what it says, that the man is the head of the house.

Use "block" quotes for longer passages.

Others highlighted the importance of adhering to tradition and the **"mores and folkways of our society"**—as one respondent put it. Another similarly indicated, "I guess it's just been the common practice for so long—the common thing to do. It's the way we did it. That's the way I think it should be done." A third group focused more on pragmatic concerns—the smooth running of day-to-day interactions and even society. As one respondent joked, women's name change **"keeps the mailman from getting confused."** All three types of responses reflect the need to turn outside of the individual for guidance on how to appropriately enact gender.

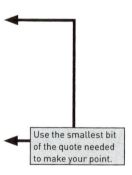

Use the smallest bit of the quote needed to make your point.

Marjorie, an African American mother of nine in Chicago, lived intermittently with Jamal, the father of her younger children. She discussed with the interviewer the difference in her partner Jamal's contributions when he lived with Marjorie versus when he was living with another woman with whom he had a concurrent relationship:

> I: So financially you said that, does he help out in a good way sometimes?
>
> M: I guess when he gets a job. Well, he bought two boxes of cereal and a gallon of milk one day. [laughing]
>
> I: . . . We've talked about the financial things, the kids. You said he helps out with watching the kids?
>
> M: Yeah, he'll help watch.
>
> I: Like when you were at work?
>
> M: Right. He'll help watch them. He'll pick them up from school.
>
> I: No problems with that?
>
> M: When he moved in with [his other girlfriend], he stopped picking them up.

Given the relatively small number of people you will likely interview or observe, it is especially important to be open to different, and potentially conflicting, interpretations of your data. As a novice, you might think that the best strategy is to pull out those quotes that support the claim you want to make (perhaps the ideas you had in mind when you designed your study) and pretend that anything contrary to that claim doesn't exist. You'd be wrong. When you gloss over inconsistencies and ignore difficult-to-explain data, you miss out on the most interesting aspects of how people see themselves and others—the real sociological stuff. Also, your professors *do not* expect your data to be so simple. As experienced sociologists who have to deal with their own messy data, they are excited when their students are able to deal intelligently with the inevitable complexity of qualitative work. When your data look *too* tidy, they have to wonder whether the data you've chosen to share accurately represent your findings. Even if most of your data do share a common feature or trend, you should look beyond those for conflicting data or other variations in those patterns.

Editing Quotations

One of the challenges of writing with quotations is getting them to fit with what you want to say. To integrate quotations into our own prose, we often need to make slight changes—to make them fit grammatically into a sentence, to add information readers will need to make sense of the quotation, to cut out some material so readers will focus their attention where we want it, and so on.

Fortunately, there is an accepted way to indicate that you have altered a quotation:

- If you *add or change* words, use square brackets.
- If you *omit* words, use ellipses.

Here are some examples. (In your own writing, don't bold bracketed parts; we did this only to highlight them for you.)

Other mothers were initially less exact in reporting health problems. For example, one ethnographer recounted her attempt to gather accurate information about one mother's health problem as follows:

She [**the mother**] told me [**the ethnographer**] that her doctor's appointment was to take care of some thyroid tumors—one big one and two small ones.... They [**the physician and nurse**] asked her if she had ever had anything done, and she told them of the transfusion after delivering her youngest son.

And this:

She couldn't always afford the medication and worried about side effects. Rena was often overwhelmed—as reflected in her self-care. Rena went to the doctor when her chest got tight, she couldn't breathe, or she was in intense pain. Otherwise, she avoided it because she "could spend $5.00 looking on the wall at Walgreen's [**buying over-the-counter remedies to self-medicate**] as opposed to a $20 co-pay for a visit to the doctor ... with working, the kids, and cleaning you don't have time to stop and listen to your body, even when there are warning signs of a problem ... you just 'do' until you can just sit in a chair and nod off."

You can also use square brackets to insert comments about interviewee emotions, inflections, gestures, and so on into a dialogue. Such descriptions can bring more life to an interview in print:

R: Is that really hard on you all when that happens?
D: Well it makes us feel bad because, well, we don't really think we're stuck-up. But like we have one big group, you know, that like we're all good friends with ... And then if you're not in something like that or you don't make it, then you just think that, you know, well, that we're *stuck-ups* [**embarrassed emphasis on last word, then laughs**] or something.

Our discussion of working with quotations in this section applies mainly to qualitative research. Although the discussion in the next section applies more extensively to quantitative work, visual displays can be used for some qualitative data, too. Qualitative researchers sometimes count instances of particular words or linguistic patterns in their interview or observation data and display them in a quantitative form. They may also treat their data statistically, calculating percentages or correlations. Because qualitative work is almost never dealing with a sample that can be generalized to a larger population, this type of quantitative treatment of qualitative data is accepted by some but not all qualitative researchers. You might want to ask your local experts (especially your professor) what they think about it. If you get the go-ahead, you'll find the following section useful for writing about your qualitative results too.

Crafting Effective Tables, Figures and Other Visuals

Many students who read research reports pay little attention to the visuals (also called *display items*)—the tables, graphs, and illustrations. They think of these things as supplemental material that they can skip over while they focus on the real stuff: the prose. You can see why this is a bad idea when you consider how experts (including your professors) read. For them, those visuals are the most important part of the report. In fact, whereas novices tend to read research reports from start to finish, barely glancing at the visuals along the way, experts often move straight from the Abstract or Introduction to the visuals and may not even read the entire paper!

So if you want your writing to be well received, you should know how to work effectively with tables, graphs, and diagrams. This work involves two related but distinct tasks and both are important: designing the visuals and discussing them in the text.

Designing the Visuals

Whether you're writing a paper or preparing a presentation, there's no reason to make visuals that can't be read or otherwise understood. And yet novices (and some who aren't!) don't seem to realize that their visuals frustrate their readers. Here are some common ways writers make interpreting their visuals difficult:

- Not including a caption or title for each visual
- Leaving out axis labels, units, or legends—or making them so small they can't be read
- Using symbols, abbreviations, or terms that the target audience won't understand. (Just because your computer program or data set used it doesn't mean it will make sense to your reader.)
- Including information not relevant for your analysis. Carefully consider everything in the visual--each column and row of a tables, each line or bar in a graph or chart. If you don't mention it, does your reader really need to see it?
- Copying and pasting output from a statistical program without selecting only relevant data or trimming to an appropriate number of significant digits
- Using an overly complicated or poorly organized layout. Does the design of your visual make it hard for readers to see important trends or make comparisons among values? For tables, can you make the reading experience easier by putting related rows or columns next to each other? For graphs, does your choice of lines or symbols make it hard to tell which is which?

To make first-rate visuals, you need to think of each one as a design problem. And just like with prose, getting them right will require rethinking and revision. Whichever kind of visual you are using, begin by taking your best shot at quickly laying it out—whether using a computer or on paper. Then imagine being someone who wants to understand it: where might they struggle to see what you want them to see? Even better, get a colleague to do a "think-aloud response" for each of your visuals. Ask him to try to understand it—saying aloud what part he is looking at and what he is thinking along the way.

Tips

Simpler is better. Only include information, data, statistics, and so on that readers need to understand the data or concept. It's fine to cut out parts of a table, as long as you don't change the actual data of what you keep.

Make it stand alone. Even though we are going to stress that you need to interpret your visuals in the text of your paper, remember the busy reader who jumps from the abstract to the visuals. Be sure that the data source, the number of observations, and labels for all important aspects of a visual are there. One of us once got the advice that if the wind blew your paper away and an expert found only one visual, she should be able to make sense of it.

Integrating Visuals and Text

Students often assume that a graph or table can stand on its own, like a painting at an art museum. But let's compare them. We *want* a work of art to invite various interpretations. A great painting may have quite different but equally powerful meanings for different viewers, and that's good. That may be part of its greatness. But when your readers see a graph or table in your sociology paper, one interpretation matters most: yours. Your readers expect you to *interpret for us*—showing us interesting trends, pointing out the most important results, and so on. As writers of science, we want to shape how our readers think about what they see when they look at our visuals. Having designed our visuals so they mean something and fit into a larger argument, we want to make sure our readers get that meaning.

Now you can understand where student writing about visuals often falls short. Your professor turns to your well-made graph, guided only by the remark, "See Figure 2." "So what?" she thinks. "*What* am I supposed to *see*? There are four curves, some go up steeply, some don't . . . some start lower, others higher . . . one is smooth, two are quite wiggly . . . What's important here?" Now imagine that she conjures you into her office with a magic spell to sit beside her while she reads your paper. When she gets to Figure 2, what do you say? Perhaps something like this: "Well, you see the solid line? That represents children from low-income families who attended Headstart. See how they start out well below the dashed lines down here, but after two years this solid line is much closer to these others up here . . . " As you speak, your professor nods . . . you can see her seeing your point.

Describing Statistical Significance

You should assume that your readers will interpret the word "significant" as shorthand for "statistically significant." Students (and journalists!) sometimes confuse *statistical significance* with the everyday meaning of *significant* as important or noteworthy. But for research writing in sociology, *statistical significance* only remarks on the likelihood that results obtained could have been due to chance given the sample that was drawn from a larger population. The degree of statistical significance is often represented by the p-value. There are two common ways of presenting p-values: stating the actual value: ($p = 0.018$) or indicating

continued

continued

the order of magnitude ($p < 0.1$) or ($p < 0.01$). Which is used depends on the specific publication—or in your case, your professor's preference. Lower values (generally less than 0.05) indicate that results were not likely due to chance alone. If you want to talk about *importance*, you'll want to use a word other than "significant" to avoid confusion. Not everything that is statistically significant is actually important to answering your research question. If you have a very large sample, tiny differences can be *statistically* significant. On the other hand, talking about a pattern that isn't statistically significant means that you *might* just be talking about chance. Be careful.

But what if you don't happen to have a professor with these particular magic powers? Then you'll need to explain your interpretation *in* your paper. How can you figure out what needs saying? For a first draft, try actually explaining each visual to someone and then writing down what you said. Need more specific ideas? Here are three common ways to "walk" your readers through your visuals:

- Identify trends—such as how the values in a row tend to decrease from left to right or perhaps stay nearly constant, or how only one of four lines has a negative slope and what that represents.
- Point out important *specifics*—extreme values in a table, the slope, peak or intercept of a line graph, and so on.
- Explain how these trends or specific values relate to the question you are addressing.

Following are examples of some visuals published in sociology journals along with the authors' discussion of those visuals. In the first example we've added the dotted arrows and ellipses to point out the moves we want you to see. Notice how each discussion draws the reader's attention to features the authors think are important (which we have highlighted in bold). Note also that the authors repeat in the text only a few key results from the visuals, and in some cases they do a little arithmetic to make it easier for readers to see the trends. As you study these examples, try to locate for yourself the specifics or trends to which the authors refer in the prose. When you're ready to do your own writing, find well-written papers with the type of visual you are using. Then *steal* the moves you need!

EXAMPLE: Chart

From Marital Name Change as a Window Into Gender Attitudes. *Gender & Society,* 2011.

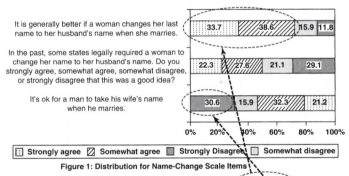

Figure 1: Distribution for Name-Change Scale Items

Figure 1 indicates that nearly three-fourths of respondents (72.3 percent) agree that it is generally better if a woman changes her last name to her husband's name when she marries. **In fact, approximately one-third of the respondents (33.7 percent) give the most conservative** response, **strongly agreeing with this statement. It is perhaps even more striking that approximately half of the respondents (49.9 percent) agree** that it was a good idea for states to legally require a woman to change her name: **in fact, nearly a quarter (22.3 percent) strongly agree** with a legal requirement. **Similarly, nearly half (46.5 percent) disagree** that is "okay" for a man to take his wife's name when he marries, **with around one-third (30.6 percent) providing the most conservative response of *strongly disagree.***

EXAMPLE: Table

From Gendered Measures, Gendered Models: Toward an Intersectional Analysis of Interpersonal Racial Discrimination. *Ethnic and Racial Studies,* 2011.

Table 1. *Percent reporting major-life racial discrimination, NSAL (N women: 2,068; N men; 1,118)*

	Men	Women	t-test	Chi-square
For unfair reasons, you have been fired?	14.67%	8.37%	***	***
For unfair reasons, you have not been hired for a job?	19.50%	11.03%	***	***
You have been unfairly denied a promotion?	18.25%	7.98%	***	***
Unfairly stopped by the police?	37.66%	8.85%	***	***
Unfairly prevented from moving into a neighborhood?	7.16%	5.90%	N/S	N/S
You have been unfairly discouraged from continuing your education?	6.35%	5.37%	N/S	N/S
Neighbors made life difficult for you or your family?	4.20%	3.09%	N/S	N/S
Have you been unfairly denied a bank loan?	7.96%	5.27%	**	**
Have you ever received service from someone such as a plumber or car mechanic that was worse than what other people get?	7.16%	2.47%	***	***

*significant at 5%c, **significant 1%c, ***significant at 0.1%

Table 1 displays the percentage of black men and black women who report having experienced particular forms of major-life racial discrimination. **Strikingly, for each of the nine measures, the percentage of** men who report having experienced discrimination **is higher than** the corresponding percentage of women. **The proportion of** men who report having been unfairly denied a promotion because of their race or ethnicity **is roughly trice the proportion of** women who report having had this experience. **Even more strikingly, the proportion of** black men who report having been unfairly stopped by the police (again because of their race) is **more than three times greater than the corresponding proportion of** black women. Men (though importantly, not women) **are more likely to** report this kind of racial discrimination than they are any of the other kinds of major-life discrimination.

EXAMPLE: Diagram

From Dangerous Liaisons? Dating and Drinking Diffusion in Adolescent Peer Networks. *American Sociological Review,* 2011.

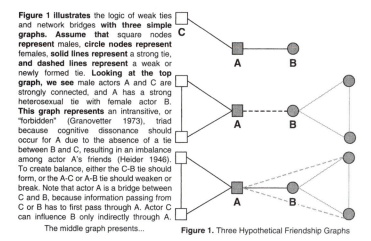

Figure 1 illustrates the logic of weak ties and network bridges **with three simple graphs. Assume that** square nodes **represent** males, **circle nodes represent** females, **solid lines represent** a strong tie, **and dashed lines represent** a weak or newly formed tie. **Looking at the top graph, we see** male actors A and C are strongly connected, and A has a strong heterosexual tie with female actor B. **This graph represents** an intransitive, or "forbidden" (Granovetter 1973), triad because cognitive dissonance should occur for A due to the absence of a tie between B and C, resulting in an imbalance among actor A's friends (Heider 1946). To create balance, either the C-B tie should form, or the A-C or A-B tie should weaken or break. Note that actor A is a bridge between C and B, because information passing from C or B has to first pass through A. Actor C can influence B only indirectly through A. The middle graph presents...

Figure 1. Three Hypothetical Friendship Graphs

EXAMPLE: Line Graph

From Dangerous Liaisons? Dating and Drinking Diffusion in Adolescent Peer Networks. *American Sociological Review,* 2011.

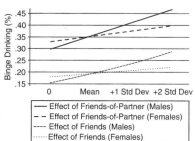

Figure 2. **Binge Drinking Predicted Probabilities** by Gender and Friends' Prior Drinking

To better illustrate the effects of friends' and friends-of-partner's drinking on future binge drinking, **Figure 2 plots** predicted probabilities of binge drinking (Model 2) **by** gender and the two friend measures. **Lines represent predicted probabilities of** male and female binge drinking across varying values of friends' and friends-of-partner's drinking, with all other variables held at their means. The gender main effect **is readily apparent;** male respondent are approximately 15 percent more likely than female respondents to binge drink when friend behaviors are held at their means. **It is also clear that** a partner's friends' drinking has strong effects on one's own probability of future binge drinking. For both boys and girls, having connections with heavy-drinking peers (i.e., two standard deviations above the mean) through a romantic partner increases the probability of binge drinking by over 25 percent compared to having no peers who drink. For direct friendships, heavy drinking friends increase the probability of binge drinking by about 10 percent compared to non-drinking friends. In addition, girls connected to a heavy drinking partner's friends are more likely to binge drink than is the average dating boy. Friends-of-partners thus provide a potential mechanism for the equalization of boys' and girls' drinking behaviors in romantic relationships.

CHECKLIST FOR WRITING RESULTS

✓ *Does the Results section contain only data and analysis?* The section should not include, for example, comparison to the findings of others or discussion of the importance or limitations of findings. Those are topics for the Discussion.

✓ *Quotations:* Is every quotation carefully chosen and edited to emphasize the words that illustrate the points you want to make? Do you explicitly state what you want readers to understand about each quote?

✓ *Illustrations:* Is every figure, table, and diagram clearly labeled and referenced in the text? Are they designed to make the important trends easy to identify? Is every illustration discussed in the text? Do you explicitly state the important trends, patterns, or values?

Writing the Discussion

You've heard the old saying about not being able to see the forest for the trees, right? Well, your job in the Discussion section is to take the readers from the trees of your Results section to a vantage point where they can perceive the forest again. At this stage, you may feel the urge to just say, "I already told you everything. This paper is so *over.*" Resist it.

In the Results, you told your readers what your findings *are.* The Discussion is your chance to explain what these findings *mean*—that is, to help your readers understand how your findings answer your research question. It's the stuff you most want your readers to remember when they stop reading your paper. The Discussion section should be the "take away" for readers.

Discussion sections often have three parts. For a short paper, each part might be only a single paragraph; for longer papers, the parts might be groups of paragraphs (perhaps labeled with subheadings). The first part is the primary and typically longest one: explaining how your findings help answer your research question. In fact, you might think of this part of the discussion as the reprise of your introduction—telling your reader how your work fills the gap you described in your introduction and how your findings compare with the prior research that you discussed.

Here is how a few expert researchers made this first move. Some started by summarizing their main conclusion in clear terms:

> People in industrialized nations tend to gain weight, at least through late midlife (Adams and Schoenborn 2006), and **our results suggest that** parenthood may steepen these weight trajectories and raise their peak. Although the difference in annual rates of gain between US parents and nonparents may not be noticeable in the short run, these differences appear to become substantial over the course of adulthood, for both women and men.

Others explicitly stated their research question again and then provided their best answer, however tentative:

> **How does coursework influence our views of the poor? Results from this study show** that whether or not an elite education can be considered a liberalizing influence on beliefs about poverty depends on both the specific type of education a student receives as well as the student's social location with respect to race and gender. Taking economics courses corresponds to higher levels of individualism, lower levels of structuralism, and lower levels of poverty alleviation policy support. Sociology and African American studies courses are associated with decreased individualism among all students.

Others backed up one step further, starting with the gap that they discovered in the literature and then stating how they filled it:

> Recently, **the literature on** college sexual relationships **has focused primarily on** the hookup culture: **Specifically, the literature has documented** negative impacts (especially on women), how heterosexual college students navigate hookups, and how casual sex has supplanted dating. **Although prior** hookup **research provides** insight into casual sexual relationships on college campuses, **it focuses too narrowly on** hookups, **excluding** the more fluid relationships that have evolved in the gap between hooking up and dating.

It's rare that any single study will completely fill a research gap. So conclusions are often qualified in some way. You should be sure to make that explicit in describing your "forest."

> **Our findings suggest that** an actor's emotional display while recounting a deviant behavior strongly influences an observer's identity inferences about that actor, and that these identity confirmation/disconfirmation inferences in turn influence sentencing judgments. **However, the results of our study indicate** that merely displaying emotion **may not** be enough to alter interactional outcomes. Neither the path analyses nor separate analyses of variance revealed a direct effect of emotion condition on sentencing outcomes.

The second major part of the Discussion is typically an acknowledgment of limitations. Being straightforward with your readers in this way can build a sense of trust with you as an author, but only if you discuss the limitations seriously.

Don't state the obvious: *every* study could have a larger sample, include additional types of people, and so on—so stating such things as limitations comes off as insincere or naive. Instead, concentrate on the limitations of your study that could really have really affected your conclusions—and suggest *how* they might have affected them. If you were using previously collected data, was there a key variable or concept that might have been important but wasn't included? A control variable that you wanted but didn't have? A variable you thought was poorly measured? Did your participant sample lack one type of people who likely would have reacted differently to the process you were studying? Would "over time" data have been optimal, but you had to settle for cross-sectional analysis due to time constraints?

Let's see how the pros do it. Here's an example of authors in our premier journal, *American Sociological Review*, acknowledging the limitations of their work:

These findings have several limitations. First, by necessity, there is a trade-off between the depth of the data we gathered through qualitative interviews and generalizability. Our respondents' experiences with the EITC may differ from those of program beneficiaries in another part of the country or recipients who receive only a small refund check. Second, there may be variation in program perceptions and allocations within the population of EITC recipients that are not obvious in a sample of only 115. Third, because our sample is not representative of welfare recipients or all wage earners, our conclusions may not speak to the meaning of welfare or wage income among people who do not receive the EITC. Perceptions and allocation of wages presumably differ, for example, among more affluent wage earners who can engage in more discretionary spending.

The final part of a Discussion is often a paragraph that describes future research that needs to be done. This part may follow fairly directly from your Limitations subsection, because new studies could be designed that eliminate some of those limitations. But they can include other things as well, because new findings almost always lead to new questions. That's why your professors publish one study after another on the same topic for decades.

Here is an example of how future research can be linked to the current question and findings:

> Thus, we find that religion shapes individuals' worldviews in ways not captured by conventional measures of religion such as denominational affiliation or religious attendance. Although religio-scientific perspectives may not correspond to all political attitudes, additional corollaries of perspectives on science and religion, including voting patterns, interpersonal behaviors, and socioeconomic attitudes, **are a promising avenue for future research. . . .**
>
> **If future research can** identify reliable ways of capturing religio-scientific perspectives using a smaller number of survey questions, these items may be worth including in other national and cross-national surveys. Such data would facilitate studying religio-scientific perspectives across domains, comparatively, and over time.

What If My Data Don't Allow Me to Answer My Question?

When you are doing research as a student, you have deadlines imposed by the school calendar. So what if, despite your best efforts, your data and/or analysis are just not working and time is running out? If you've made a sincere effort along the way, don't panic. Your professor or mentor should understand this outcome.

If you come to the point where there's just no more time to continue your research and you still don't have conclusive results, you need to shift to an alternate plan. Our advice wouldn't work in the professional world but often makes sense for school projects that have a nonnegotiable end point: Present the results you've got clearly; then, in your Discussion, state the outcome of your analyses as best you can, and then explain what you think went wrong and why. End by describing what you would do to correct the problem if you had time to back up and try again. This last part is essential, transforming your experimental failure into a meaningful learning experience—which is the purpose of the assignment, right?

If you think you may be headed for this alternate ending, have a chat with your instructor well before time runs out, and before you begin writing the Discussion. Make sure your mentor agrees with your plan, and clarify your understanding of what would be appropriate in explaining the unfortunate outcome.

Here's the beginning of the Discussion section from the paper of a student who had such a problem. She earned an A+!

> The results of this experiment are decidedly inconclusive. The data do not show any relationship between a subject's affective distance to a priming target identity and the ease with which the subject can be primed.
>
> However, this lack of relationship seems to have occurred because of underlying problems in the experimental procedure rather than weaknesses in the theory or reasoning underlying the experiment. There are several indications of failures in the experimental procedure. First, the education level of respondents . . .

CHECKLIST FOR DISCUSSION SECTION

✓ Do you explain how your findings relate to your research question and to the most relevant prior research that you discussed in your literature review?

✓ Do you discuss both the strengths and limitations of your contribution?

✓ Do you map out an agenda for research?

Writing Abstracts

You probably read lots of abstracts while you were trying to decide on a research question and while you were constructing your Theory/Literature Review section. If you found it frustrating when you couldn't tell the research question—or its answer—from the abstract, don't do that to *your* reader. Also, remember that the Abstract is the first thing that your readers will read. It's your first, best chance to make a good impression and communicate the importance and quality of your paper.

> Most research-based writing assignments should have some kind of summary. For a short research paper, the abstract might be only three to four sentences. If you are doing a case study or an internship report (see Chapter 2), you'd do an *executive summary* instead. If you write a research proposal, you'd be expected to start it with a *project summary*.

So once you've written a complete draft of your paper, it's time to go back to the beginning. Your abstract will need to summarize your entire project in less than a page. To the novice, abstracts often seem like an extra and uninteresting step required before turning in a finished research report. To experts, abstracts are among the most important kinds of writing that researchers produce. Sociologists read many more abstracts than they do actual papers. Because more research gets published than anyone has the time (or interest) to read, sociologists read abstracts just to keep abreast of what's going on in areas that might impact their own. They also use abstracts as a screening tool to decide which articles are relevant enough to read. Because they know that the abstract is such an important first impression, experts usually spend more time revising their abstract than any other single paragraph in their paper.

To help you learn the art of writing abstracts, let's start with some clear and simple guidelines—reproduced here from the American Sociological Association (ASA) website.

ASA Guide to Writing an Informative Abstract

Please write an informative abstract. Be orderly, succinct, and concrete. Use active verbs such as "report," "propose," and "analyze" rather than static verbs such as "is," "are," and "appears to be." Do not hedge or equivocate. Abstracts should be less than 200 words.

OBJECTIVE: State the core issue, research question, or objective of the research.

METHODS: Briefly describe the methods, including the population, sampling method, sample size, study design (e.g., survey, experiment or in-depth interview study), and the date of the data collection.

RESULTS: Describe the results.

CONCLUSIONS: Interpret the results as supporting or not supporting the theory or hypotheses. Draw conclusions and state implications.

These are useful tips. But sociologists don't necessarily follow this template exactly—which means that your professor may prefer something a bit different. Next we present a few common variations. For your own research project, you might find that one is a better fit than another. You may also want to show these variations to your professor and ask if she has a preference.

Model #1: topic > gap > findings

In the 1980s and 1990s, single-disease interest groups emerged as an influential force in U.S. politics. This article explores their effects on federal medical research priority-setting. Previous studies of advocacy organizations' political effects focused narrowly on direct benefits for constituents. Using data on 53 diseases over 19 years, I find that in addition to securing direct benefits, advocacy organizations have aggregate effects and can systemically change the culture of policy arenas. Disease advocacy reshaped funding distributions, changed the perceived beneficiaries of policies, promoted metrics for commensuration, and made cultural categories of worth increasingly relevant to policymaking.

Introduce topic

Establish gap

Present findings

Model #2: topic > gap > aims > findings

Commitment highlights one of the ways in which individuals infuse roles and social structure with self-motivated behaviors, thereby linking the self to social structure. Past theoretical formulations of commitment, including work by Becker, Stryker, and Kanter, tended to focus on commitment as a tie between an individual and either 1) a line of activity, 2) particular role

Introduce topic

Establish gap

continued

partners, or 3) an organization. An approach based on identity theory or affect control theory (each of which uses a cybernetic model of identity processes) suggests that commitment connects an individual to an identity. In this view, commitment does not link a person to consistent lines of activity, other role partners, or organizations, but to a stable set of self-meanings. These stable self-meanings, in turn, produce consistent lines of activities. This idea is borne out in an analysis of data from the college student role, in which there exist multiple, independent bases of commitment containing cognitive and socioemotional components. Commitment moderates the relationship between student identity and role performance such that the relationship is stronger for persons with higher commitment.

Describe aims of present work

Summarize findings

Model #3: topic > methods > aims > findings> implications

Strong child support enforcement requires fathers to take financial responsibility for their children and may also encourage more responsible sexual behavior. Using the 1997–2001 waves of the 1997 National Longitudinal Survey of Youth (N = 4,272), this article examines the association between child support enforcement and the sexual activity of male adolescents. Stronger child support enforcement was associated with fewer sexual partners, less frequent sexual intercourse, and a higher likelihood of using contraceptive methods among adolescents who had had sexual intercourse in the 12 months preceding data collection. The effects of child support enforcement were particularly strong for non-White adolescents and those living in high-poverty areas. These findings suggest that strengthening child support enforcement may be associated with reductions in some aspects of male adolescents' sexual activity.

Introduce topic

Briefly describe data collection and sample

State research question/agenda

Briefly summarize findings

Briefly summarize implications

continued

Model #4: gap > methods > findings > implications

Studies examining determinants of divorce have largely ignored differences between factors that elevate wives' and husbands' initiation of divorce.	Establish gap
The authors use longitudinal data and a latent class model embedded in a competing-risks event history model to assess distinct predictors of wives and husbands leaving marriages.	Describe methods and aims of present work
They find that when men are not employed, either spouse is more likely to leave. When wives report better-than-average marital satisfaction, their employment affects neither spouse's exit. However, when wives report below-average marital satisfaction, their employment makes it more likely they will leave.	Briefly summarize findings
The authors' findings suggest that theories of divorce require "gendering" to reflect asymmetric gender change.	Briefly summarize implications

Creating a Title

You may want to start thinking about a title when you come up with your research question, but you won't finalize it until the very last stage of your writing. That's because it should evoke that broad forest that you were describing in your Discussion section, and you won't know that until you've done your analysis and described it for your reader.

There are several strategies for writing a good title. One is to state the question that you will answer, in short form. For example, the paper on parenthood and obesity could have been titled: "Does Parenthood Lead to Weight Gain?" The actual title of that paper took a different approach—announcing its general topic first and then focusing on the major variables that are related in the analysis: "Parenthood and Trajectories of Change in Body Weight Over the Life Course." Some authors combine the approaches, starting with a topic and following with a more specific question: "Getting a Job: Is There a Motherhood Penalty?" The order can be reversed, of course: "Gender Bias or Motherhood Disadvantage? Judgments of Blue-Collar Mothers and Fathers in the Workplace." Sometimes titles focus on the findings rather than the question. This isn't so common in sociology as in some other sciences, but perhaps it should be when findings are definitive; it lets the reader see the bottom line instantly. For example, a recent paper that was titled "Is Obesity Contagious? Social Networks Versus Environmental Factors in the Obesity Epidemic" could have been called "Obesity Is Not Contagious If You Control for Contextual Effects."

You might notice that a lot of our title examples involve two parts: a title and subtitle. It's really tempting to do that because you want to cram as much into that first contact with the reader as you can. But at least one excellent sociologist, Chuck Tilly, has argued against subtitles. He never wrote a book that had a subtitle; he thought that you should think hard about what the title should be and not cheat by effectively having two titles. If we could write great titles like he did, that would be excellent advice. Some of his best were "Durable Inequality," "From Mobilization to Revolution," and "Stories, Identities and Political Change." The most cited article that one of the authors here ever wrote had a cryptic title, "Birds of a Feather," referring to the topic of homophily (the tendency of people to associate with others who are like themselves); the reference is to an Aesop Fable in which a stork that hung out with crows suffered for its bad company. So sometimes you can get away with being creative. If you do something unusual like that, make very, very sure that your abstract is clear and professional!

Now that we've been through the basics of writing a full research paper based on original research, let's look at some of the issues that will come up again and again in your writing. Chapters 7, 8, and 9 look at sources and style issues that will be important in every type of sociological writing that you do.

CHOOSING AND USING SOURCES

7

Most of the papers you write for your sociology courses will require sources, and different assignments require different types of sources. But your decisions about sources go far beyond selecting the right type. For a good paper, you'll need to pay close attention to the quality and applicability of the sources, and you'll need to know how to use them effectively. We'll cover these topics in this chapter. In Chapter 8 we cover other aspects of source use, especially the mechanics of citation and strategies for avoiding plagiarism.

Ways to Use Sources

We'll start by helping you understand some basic ways sociologists *use* sources. Knowing how you plan to use a source will help you make smarter choices and maybe save you time as well.

In the humanities, scholars often talk about sources as being either *primary* or *secondary*. However, because sociologists study people (or data about people) rather than texts, this terminology isn't very useful. And besides, a writer can use the same kind of source in very different ways. To help you learn how sociologists work with sources, we've developed a vocabulary adapted from a taxonomy developed by Joseph Bizup. Our four categories for using sources are *Background* (B), *Argument* (A), *Method* (M), and *Theory* (T).

Background Source

A *background* source provides factual stuff. We frequently use these in introduction sections to help readers understand a topic or idea, or show why something is interesting or important. We're also using sources as background when we provide statistics, definitions, and so on. Basically, you are using a source as background when you expect your readers to accept the information you provide without question. If you cite a source to say, "You can trust me on this because it says so here," it's background. In the examples of background sources that follow, notice how the information cited is presented in a matter-of-fact way:

According to 2009 Monitoring the Future data, the 30-day prevalence of self-reported drunkenness is over five times higher among 12th graders (27.4 percent) than among 8th graders (5.4 percent) (Johnston et al. 2009).

During and following the protest cycle of the 1960s and 1970s, the constitutional protections afforded to public gatherings in the United States with the intent to "petition the government" were widened and specified (Gora et al. 1991; McWhirter 1994).

In 1994, the Senate appropriations committee ordered the NIH to submit a report of funding by death rates, medical spending, and diseases' indirect economic costs (Agnew 1996). That same year, the Congressional Research Service produced a report of NIH funding and mortality rates for the leading causes of death (Johnson 1994).

Primary and Secondary Sources

You might hear sources referred to as *primary* or *secondary*. These terms can be confusing because they mean different things in different disciplines. In fields like history or literature that primarily interpret texts, these terms are used frequently. For those folks, primary sources are the things they interpret—poems, films, private journals, government documents, and so on. But sociologists don't often refer to sources as primary or secondary. If they do, primary refers to reports of original research—the articles your sociology professors publish in journals like *American Journal of Sociology* and *Family Relations*. These are papers in which the scientists themselves present their new research. Their intended audience is other researchers in the field, along with professionals in government or policy work who draw on sociological knowledge. If sociologists talk about secondary sources, they're referring to writing about primary sources; this might include review articles that summarize recent research conducted by others on a particular sociological topic. If you write a literature review for a class, you're producing a kind of secondary source.

Argument Source

You use sources as *argument* when you provide readers with evidence or reasons relevant to your claims. Argument sources might support your claim, as in the following example where the author claims that in the 1980s, "virtually every disease could use measures of dollars per death or per patient to claim their disease was underfunded compared to HIV/AIDS":

For example, in 1984, breast cancer advocate Rose Kushner testified that the federal government was spending $11,000 for each new AIDS patient but only $400 per person diagnosed with breast cancer (U.S. Congress 1984:49).

Here's another example. In this one, the source is presented as a direct (block) quotation:

In the report, the NIH for the first time listed criteria for priority-setting between diseases. They provided five un-ranked criteria:

public health needs, scientific quality of the research, potential for scientific progress (the existence of promising pathways and qualified investigators), portfolio diversification along the broad and expanding frontiers of research, and adequate support of infrastructure (human capital, equipment instrumentation, and facilities). (Institute of Medicine 1998:4)

These criteria provide some information about NIH priority-setting while maintaining significant scientific autonomy over funding decisions.

An argument source can also be a stand-in for a person or group espousing a point of view or making a claim about something relevant to your own argument—whether you agree with it or not: "So-and-so says . . . " In our trial analogy, this would be like a defense attorney saying, "The state's attorney wants you to believe that my client . . . " An argument source may state the point or claim explicitly, or it may imply a position or claim. If you believe the point to be valid and relevant, and if you believe your readers will accept the source as a legitimate authority, you will use the source to support your claim. If you think a source is relevant but has questionable merit, you can cite it in order to argue *against* it. (For detailed instructions on this kind of source use, see Concessions and Counterarguments, pp. 224–228)

You may also use argument sources to show readers the range of positions that are held, which is often they way they are used in Introduction and Literature Review sections of research reports. When used for this purpose, sources are often clustered to show a common and therefore important position:

> **Scholars have argued** that disease advocates successfully lobbied for research funds (Brown and Zavestoski 2004; Dresser 1999; Epstein 1996).

Multiple argument sources can also be contrasted with one another, especially to represent commonly held ideas or positions:

> **Peer selection theorists argue** that substance use is thus an antecedent, not a consequence, of friendship formation (**Gottfredson and Hirschi 1990; Hirschi 1969**). On the other hand, **theories of peer influence suggest** that friendship groups provide intimate settings for individuals to learn behaviors and attitudes, including those related to substance use (**Akers 2009; Bandura 1977; Sutherland 1947**).

An *argument* source may also be used to provide contrast for your own work:

> **Most existing research** treats target populations as a constant feature of policies, often coding the target population directly from the text of bills (Donovan 2001; Schroedel

and Jordan 1998). **In contrast, I argue that** a policy's perceived targets can change over time.

Theory Source

Theory sources basically do what it seems: They provide references to sociological theories or ideas. The sociological world is a complex place, and we can only apply a limited number of sociological ideas or concepts in any single piece of writing. Theory sources show our readers the theoretical lens we are using in discussing our topic or designing our study.

The theory sources sociologists use can usually be sorted into two types. "Classic" (or canonical) sources provide the deep background, connecting the new work to the major ideas and theorists of the field. Contemporary sources, in contrast, are more directly related to the sociologist's current research. In the next example, the authors begin with a reference to the original classic source of the theoretical ideas, which sets up their discussion of more recent research:

> A long tradition of sociological work relates remedial actions by norm violators to how social observers perceive them. Goffman (1971) gave perhaps the most compelling picture of the impression management that is needed after an offense. . . . As Goffman (1971:113) put it, "an apology is a gesture through which an individual splits himself into two parts, the part that is guilty of an offense and the part that dissociates itself from the illicit and affirms a belief in the offended rule . . . "
>
> Apologies are effective in reducing anger toward transgressors, and in reducing how much observers wish to punish them (see, e.g., Darby and Schlenker 1982; Ohbuchi et al. 1989; Riordan et al. 1983). Only recently, studies have begun to explore more carefully which facets of apology

work to reduce sanctions and the mechanisms through which these apologies work. Scher and Darley (1997b) demonstrate that an expression of remorse had a significant impact in reducing [sanctions].

Sometimes papers will have a distinct "Theory" section. More often the theory is interwoven with discussion of other research. (This is typically the case for student research reports.) Regardless of where in the source it appears, when you are talking about the *sociological ideas* behind your hypotheses or interpretation of results, you're using that source to provide theoretical framing for your paper.

Method Source

You use method sources to show that a procedure or approach *you* use in your own work is similar to what someone else did. As a writer, citing a *method* source helps you in two ways: First, if someone else has described in detail something that you are doing, you don't need to describe it in detail again; just give a brief summary and then direct your readers to that source. Second, if you cite a method source that your readers judge to be authoritative and relevant, they will have more confidence in what you're doing.

Not surprisingly, *method* sources are most likely to show up in the Methods section. These sources explain or justify why you did what you did, like this:

Following a study by the General Accounting Office (1997), I have assumed that the best estimate of the potential donor pool is the in-hospital death rate adjusted for circumstance or cause of death.

However, if a particular procedure or approach is central to your research project rather than just a detail, you may want to mention it briefly (and cite it) in your Introduction:

We use a two-equation estimation procedure (**based on Heckman 1976**) to address self-selection into relationships and offending.

And if it makes it into your Intro, it may also be worthy of discussing at some length in the Literature Review/Theory section.

A *method* source may also supply definitions, categories, or labels that you will use for your own work:

Recent work on demeanor and the police use of force (**Engel, Sobal, and Worden 2000; Garner, Maxwell, and Heraux 2002**) has distinguished two important dimensions of disrespectful behavior: disrespectful demeanor toward an officer and the use of physical force against an officer.

Citations to databases are also a type of *method* sources:

We test our hypotheses using two waves of data from the National Longitudinal Study of Adolescent Health (**Add Health, 2001**).

Four Ways to Use Sources in Sociology Writing: A Summary

Background: To reference information as facts. "You don't have to take my word for it; you can look it up here."

Argument: To present evidence supporting (or challenging) your claim. "Should we believe

continued

continued

> X? Let's consider this . . ." Or to present
> someone else's position or claim and respond
> to it: "So-and-so says . . . "
>
> *Theory*: To provide a sociological framework or
> lens for your ideas, interpretations, or research
>
> *Method*: To borrow a procedure or approach. "I
> didn't invent this way of doing X. You can read
> about it here."

Quoting, Paraphrasing, and Summarizing

Once you have decided to use a source for a particular purpose, you need to decide *how* to use it. Your three main choices are these:

- *Quoting*: repeating the sources words exactly (or with slight, clearly noted edits)
- *Paraphrasing*: restating the ideas or information using about the same amount of space but reworded to make it fit your own purpose and context
- *Summarizing*: describing or explaining something in far fewer words than the original (this may also include explaining the overall point of a chart or table in words)

Whichever you choose, it's important to keep your own voice out front. In other words, readers should feel that they are hearing *your* perspective even when you are discussing the work of other writers. Here are some guidelines on how to deploy your sources effectively.

Quote Only When the Exact Words Matter

When readers encounter a quotation in your paper, they assume there is something important about the exact words used in the source that you want them to notice. Readers will pay special attention to those quoted words—in order to see what you think is so important. So if the exact words of your source aren't important, putting them in quotes is a misleading signal; in that case, you should paraphrase or summarize instead.

When Quoting, Use the Fewest Words Possible

We understand why you might be tempted to use the longest possible excerpt. (We too can recall high school assignments for which we inflated our two pages of ideas to fill the required ten-page minimum.) But when you use more of someone else's words than you need to make your point, it makes it harder for readers to see in those words what you want them to see. If a quotation includes more than is needed, readers—including your professor—are well aware that you are wasting space (and their time). When we asked our colleagues for their pet peeves regarding student writing, overlong quotes came up often.

Quote Only the Words Needed to Make Your Point

Instead of this . . .

In "Bourgeois and Proletarians," the first section of the Manifesto, Marx argues that the history of society is the history of unceasing class struggles: **"Freeman and slave, patrician and plebeian, lord and serf, guild-master and journeyman, in a word, oppressor and oppressed, stood in constant opposition to one another, carried on an uninterrupted, now hidden, now open fight, a fight that each time ended, either in**

continued

continued

a revolutionary re-constitution of society at large, or in the common ruin of the contending classes."

. . . write this:

In the first section of the Manifesto, "Bourgeois and Proletarians," Marx argues that the history of society is the history of unceasing class struggles: **"Freeman and slave, patrician and plebeian, lord and serf, guild-master and journeyman, in a word, oppressor and oppressed."**

Keep Your Voice Out in Front: It's Your Paper

Your readers need to feel that everything in the paper is being shaped by your brain, even when you're discussing what other people wrote or said.

Here is one dependable technique for making your paper read like *your* paper: Start every section and most paragraphs with an introduction in which you share your own points, ideas, or perspectives—before discussing what others have said or thought. For a paragraph, this introduction will usually require a sentence at least. For the start of a section, you might need a paragraph. (Note: these are minimums. If you start every paragraph with only a sentence of your own and then fill the rest of the paragraph with source material, you're still patchwriting! See Chapter 8, pp. 192–194.) If you tend to make your points at the ends of paragraphs, try shifting them to the beginning.

Here is another way to keep your voice out front: When you discuss a source at some length, refer to the author (or organization) by name to make them characters in your paper. It might seem odd that you can make your work more your own by naming other people, but it's true. When you write,

"According to Durkheim . . ." we hear you speaking; but if you just summarize Durkheim without explicitly attributing his ideas to him—your voice gets muddled with his. Here are guidelines for when to invoke an author directly in your prose:

- If you are quoting, *always* invoke the author(s) by name in addition to the citation. If the exact words are important, who said them must also be important.
- If you are summarizing or paraphrasing ideas, concepts, arguments, or reasons that you can attribute to specific authors or organizations, bring them into your discussion.
- If you use a reference as a source for statistics, dates, definitions, or other information that you expect readers to accept without question as plain facts, the citation alone is sufficient. Here's another way to look at it: If you could just as well have found the same information in other sources, the author probably isn't important enough to mention directly.

Altering a Quotation

There are times when the exact words of a source are important enough to quote, but you need to change them just a bit. Say the sentence you want to quote is in the middle of a paragraph, and it uses a pronoun to refer to someone named at the start of the paragraph. If you leave it as it is, your readers won't understand it because they don't know what the pronoun refers to. You could quote everything from the start of the paragraph to the sentence you want, but, as we explain above, all of those extra words make it harder for your readers to get the point of the quotation. Your best options is to change the quotation by replacing the pronoun with its antecedent—using square brackets to show where you altered the quotation. Square brackets are a signal to your readers telling them, "I've done some editing to this quotation and I want you to know exactly what I've changed."

In the following example, the quoted material originally began a sentence and so the first letter was capitalized. But since the author wanted to imbed the material into the middle of her own sentence, she changed the first letter to lowercase, identifying the alteration with brackets:

> One is not surprised to find leading eugenicists proselytizing, as when Karl Pearson suggested that "[s]**ocialists** have to inculcate that spirit which would give offenders against the State short shrift and the nearest lamp-post."

If additional words are needed to make a quoted passage understandable because it has been removed from its context, use square brackets:

> "Most Jews only secured a stable position in the low and middling ranks of the bourgeoisie at the end of the [**nineteenth**] century" (Hyman 1998:62), . . .
>
> Sutherland argued that "the fallacy of the proposed method [**regarding the minimum wage**] of attaining it is that it assumes that every employer is bound in all events to furnish it."

You can also use square brackets to eliminate unnecessary words. In the following example, the author has omitted many words in the middle of the passage that weren't relevant to her point. When she picks up again after the ellipsis, only a pronoun (they) is need to identify the subject from the first part of the quotation:

> "Expert policy counsel, in fact, turned out to be the ground on which laissez-faire's professional critics regrouped and refashioned a position of influence . . . [**they**] established

new forms of authority by colonizing the social space between university professorships and expert government service."

Summarizing Versus Paraphrasing

If you don't have a good reason to quote a source, your choices are summarizing or paraphrasing. When should you paraphrase? When you want to capture the essential details of a sentence or longer passage, but either the exacting wording isn't important or the language used in the source isn't a good fit for your context. For example, say you want to include a description of how a study was conducted, but the authors of the study used highly technical language that your readers probably won't understand. Think of paraphrasing as a type of translation: The authors of the source were writing for their context, which is not the same as yours. You want to rewrite the passage in a way that is faithful to the original but in words that make sense for the writing you are doing.

When should you summarize? When you want to tell your readers about something you read in a source, but in less detail than the original. You might reduce a full paragraph to a sentence or two, or perhaps capture the gist of an entire section or chapter in a few sentences. You might even have occasion to explain the main point of an entire book in a paragraph. Because you are reducing the amount of prose, you want to focus on what's important *for your purpose*.

Dealing With Jargon in Summary Writing

Students often pay insufficient attention to the words they choose when writing summaries. Once you have a draft of your summary, step back and look for specialized

continued

continued

vocabulary—words, phrases, abbreviations, or acronyms that someone without specialized knowledge wouldn't likely understand. For each item you identify, ask yourself these questions: Is this important for my paper? Do I use it more than once or twice? Unless you can clearly answer "yes" to both questions, it's not reasonable to make your reader learn them. Replace those words with language your readers will understand.

This doesn't mean that you should always avoid using technical language. It's often reasonable—especially if avoiding such terms makes your writing longwinded and repetitive. But remember that you may need to teach or remind *your* readers what these words mean—even if that wasn't true for readers of the source text. If that's the case, take the time to do it right: Define those terms, spell out the acronyms, and so on. If you think you'll need more than a few sentences or it seems to interrupt the flow of your writing, do it in a footnote.

Students are often given assignments to summarize a text without any *context*. This is a nonsensical assignment. There is no such thing as a well-written summary *in general*. The amount of detail you need to include and the words you should use are entirely dependent on who you are writing for and why. If you are writing for specialists in a particular subfield of sociology, you could effectively summarize a research report in a few sentences. You'd need to use more space and less technical language to communicate effectively with sociologists who work outside of that area, and considerably more words and less jargon if your readers are not trained in sociology at all.

So if you are asked to write a summary, ask for the context: Who is the summary for? Why would they be reading it? Once you have a sense of your rhetorical context, use it to guide your decisions. Ask yourself, "What do *my* readers need to know? Which details might have been important for readers of the source text but are not relevant for my readers?"

Choosing Sources

Although you will use many different types of sources in writing sociology papers, we think the most important distinction is between these three categories:

1. *Theoretical work*: These are writings that focus on the how and why of sociology. They provide the ideas that guide how we understand the field, the questions we ask, and how we interpret data we collect.
2. *Research reports:* These are the papers (and sometimes books) written by researchers presenting new research— what they did, how they did it, and what they think it means. Research reports are the source of our knowledge regarding how people actually interact.
3. Everything else

We are going to skip over the first category—because (1) this is a short book and (2) for almost everything you will write in sociology courses, your professors will assign or guide you to the relevant theoretical material. If you need help choosing theoretical sources, ask your instructor.

Peer-Reviewed Studies: The Gold Standard

For research literature, there is one quality your professors will likely consider more important than anything else: whether or not it's *peer reviewed*. Like all sciences, sociology has an established quality-control mechanism for published research. Despite the high quality of much sociological research, there's some dubious and substandard stuff, too—papers that "talk" like research but are really just biased advocacy pieces with cherry-picked data. Sorting out the quality and value of new research is the function of the peer review system.

Peer review functions something like movie reviews you've probably read or watched. Viewers won't all agree on whether a particular movie is great, but if reviewers for *The New York Times*, *The New Yorker*, and *The Los Angeles Times* all give a movie the "thumbs up," it's very unlikely to be a bad film. For research journals, editors send articles to (typically) three scholars who are specialists in the subfield of the submitted article. Each of them independently reviews the article and sends comments privately back to the editor. Based on these reviews, the editor decides whether to (1) accept the article as is, (2) ask the authors to "revise and resubmit," or (3) reject the paper. A paper will be rejected if it doesn't meet the quality standards of the journal, but also if the editor doesn't believe that the topic or approach is a good fit with the journal's mission. Many papers now go through multiple rounds of revision before getting accepted. (Yes, your professors usually have to revise their writing, too!) Peer review isn't perfect; reviewers and editors are human and thus prone to errors and biases like the rest of us. But it's the best filter we've got.

The number of peer-reviewed journals that publish sociologically relevant research is quite large, and there's a definite pecking order among them. Although there is no single accepted measure for determining which journals are "best," every professional sociologist would recognize a few as decidedly top tier: *American Journal of Sociology*, *American Sociological Review*, and *Annual Review of Sociology*. Publishing in these journals gives authors the greatest prestige and visibility, and reviewers for articles are chosen from among the top experts. If a well-conducted database search turns up way too many relevant hits, one way to select among them is by journal reputation. When in doubt, *ask your librarian*; it will be his favorite question of the day. Of course, you can ask your professors, too. And if you are inquiring as to whether a particular source is acceptable, you can also ask for suggestions for better sources. Professors are usually happy to help students who have done some serious work on their own first.

Top Journals in Sociology

There are more highly respected journals in the field than we have space to mention, but here are some of them:

American Journal of Sociology	*American Sociological Review*
Annual Review of Sociology	*Rationality and Society*
Sociological Methodology	*Sociological Methods &*
Sociology of Education	*Research, Population and*
Social Networks	*Development Review*
Social Problems	*Social Forces*
Law & Society Review	*Journal of Marriage and Family*
Gender & Society	*Sociological Theory*
Social Science Research	*Theory and Society*
Social Psychology Quarterly	*Journal for the Scientific Study*
	of Religion

Other Types of Sources

Many of your sociology writing tasks will require the use of scholarly literature, the kind of sources we discussed earlier. But for most projects, you will need to use other kinds of sources as well. The types of sources you need will depend on the kind of writing you are doing—but just because a source is the right *type* doesn't automatically mean it's a good choice. This is true for any writing you do, but it's especially important in sociology. The topics sociologists study are often related to hot-button issues on which people have strong opinions and may also have major policy implications—things like racial and gender equality, adolescent behavior, education, public safety, and so on. Strong opinions and policy ramifications can lead to biased presentation of facts, data, and research. Another complexity is that key facts central to some sociology topics can change markedly in only a few years. (Just one year before we began this book, marijuana was not legal for recreational use anywhere in the United States.) This means that we have to be especially careful in choosing our sources. A savvy consideration of sources will consider three factors: *timeliness, authoritativeness,* and *bias.*

Timeliness: Does It Pass the Sniff Test?

A fresh piece of salmon will start to smell unpleasant after just a few days. When does a source begin to stink? That depends on the nature of the material *and* how you plan to use it. If you're discussing sociological theory, Durkheim's *The Division of Labour in Society* could be quite relevant, even though it was published in 1893. But some sources become outdated for some purposes within a few years or even sooner. Consider this citation from a sociology paper on online dating:

> The Match.com website has more than twelve million members (Gibbs 2006).

Note that this paper cites the Gibbs source as *current* information: "Match.com <u>has</u> . . . " Is it likely that the membership of a match-making website could change dramatically in just a few years? Of course. So while this citation would have been just fine for a paper written in 2006 or 2007, it reeks now. On the other hand, if you are investigating how online dating has *changed over time*, Gibbs might always be a good reference for a 2006 benchmark.

So you see, you can't judge the freshness of a source without considering *how* you use it. There's no simple answer to the question, "How old is too old?" You have to use your brain and your nose. Good theory is like good red wine; it lasts a very long time. A statistic describing how things *are* is more like fresh fish. Research findings are somewhere in-between (perhaps an onion?), since their current value depends a lot on how much related research has been done since they were published. If you cite a research report as gospel that's since been refuted by many studies, it will be clear that you haven't done your homework. On the other hand, citing an older but groundbreaking study that started the line of work you are discussing is useful for showing your reader the foundation for your thinking.

Authoritativeness: Do They Have the Credentials?

Imagine you are 5 years old, and Jimmy, the 7-year-old kid from across the street, tells you it's okay to let his dog lick your mouth. His dog's mouth, he tells you, is cleaner than your own. Does the 5-year-old you pause to reflect on the source of this information? ("Let's see . . . What kind of background would someone need to know such facts? A veterinary degree? Or a master's degree in public health?") Not likely. Five-year-old you is equally unlikely to judge Jimmy's veracity on the dog-licking statement based on what he told you in the past ("If you make a funny face and keep it that way for more than 5 minutes, it will stay that way forever"). It's doubtful you'd even have

FIGURE 7.1 Consider whether your source is authoritative.

paused to consider what that tongue was licking just before it got to your mouth.

When we say that a source should be *authoritative,* we mean that those providing the material are authorities on the specific subject matter at hand. Do you go to Jimmy to find out where you can find a red crayon in his house? Sure. To get facts about canine–human pathogen transfers? No way. You need to be similarly judicious in choosing whose information or opinion you want in your papers.

For peer-reviewed journal articles, authoritativeness isn't really an issue. You can assume that the journal editor has taken care of that. But for other types of sources, you need to ask, "Is *this* a good source for *that* information?" If it's facts you're after, you'd do better to start with this question: "Given what I want to know, who is most likely to have that expertise?" Then use your answer (or your librarian's answer) to locate an authoritative source.

Choosing Sources

- *Is it timely?* Give it the sniff test. Decide whether sources are sufficiently up to date.

- *Is it authoritative?* Check its credentials. Use sources you and your reader will trust.
- *Is it biased?* Interrogate it. Know who is behind your sources and be skeptical about their motivations.

When it comes to judging whether a source is suitably authoritative, you're not the only one whose opinion matters. You should expect your readers to be skeptical, too. Your Aunt Mimi may actually know quite a bit about what makes women more likely to return to prison once they are out on parole, but your readers will have more faith in your writing if you cite the US Department of Justice's Bureau of Justice Statistics. Use sources that you *and* your readers will accept.

Here are a few tips for judging authoritativeness. In the age of Google, it's usually easy to figure these things out with a little poking around.

- Who wrote it and what are their credentials? What do you know about the author or publisher? If it's a webpage, be especially careful, since anybody can build a website and make it look professional.
- Government agencies may not be inherently reliable sources for all information, but they're a safer bet than randomly chosen sites. If you're looking for something that a government agency might publish, limit your search to .gov sites. (On Google, just add site:.gov to your search.)
- Don't confuse databases with publishers. The fact that you find an article via EBSCO or Elsevier doesn't tell you anything about how authoritative specific sources are for your purpose.

Bias: Are There Conflicts of Interest?

In a class one of us taught some years ago, students were researching whether modern electric toothbrushes were more effective than the old-fashioned, hand-powered kind. There were about a dozen peer-reviewed articles on the topic, and *every* one included either an author who worked for a toothbrush manufacturer or had funding from such a company. This doesn't mean such studies are worthless; but it would be easy to miss this important information if you weren't looking for it. And it matters: There are many ways to measure toothbrush "effectiveness," and some are more likely to produce favorable outcomes than others. The same is true for determining whether violent crime is increasing, if dispensing clean needles increases drug use, or whether abstinence-only education reduces teen pregnancy.

Depending on what you're studying, there may or may not be such obvious conflicts of interest at work. But it's important to understand who might have a stake in the various sources of information you are using. Let's say you are studying whether police tend to use excessive force in certain situations. Whose data should you rely on? The police? The libertarian think tank CATO? An activist group? There is no such thing as a completely unbiased source, but some are clearly more biased than others. Although we can't always know why a source presents data one way rather than another, a sophisticated person will do some digging if she doesn't have good reason to trust a particular source. (Librarians are good at this, too.)

If you find that various sources provide contradictory information, don't despair. Instead, recognize that you have uncovered something important about the way that information is disseminated. That is in itself worth explaining to your readers.

A Note About Wikipedia

Wikipedia is certainly great for source snooping, but many professors don't consider it to be an appropriate source for academic papers (even though studies have shown Wikipedia to be equal in quality to the standard encyclopedias).

Snooping Sources With Wikipedia

1. Find the name of the publisher or hosting organization. Don't cite any source—whether periodical, book, or website—that doesn't name the organization or publisher.
2. Check the name of the organization or publisher in Wikipedia. Nothing there? Be very skeptical.
3. Skim the Wikipedia entry to get a feel for whether the source can be considered reasonably authoritative and to assess biases.
4. If the source passes the authoritativeness test but seems likely to have a strong bias on the matter at hand, ask a librarian to help you find other sources to consider alongside this one. At a minimum, comment on the likely bias when you discuss the material from source in your paper.

Let's say you want to know whether home-schooled children have more or less success in college compared to other kids. A quick look on the Web turns up many hits, including information from these three organizations:

1. National Home Education Research Institute (NHERI)
2. *Journal of College Admission*
3. The Cato Institute

Let's do the Wikipedia snoop. The first is quick: no entry for NHERI, so that one doesn't pass our test. What about the *Journal of College Admission*? The website for the journal gives its parenting organization as the National Association for College Admission Counseling—which does have a Wikipedia entry; we learn this is "an organization of more than 13,000 professionals from around the world dedicated to serving students transitioning from secondary to post-secondary education. It includes professional school counselors, college access counselors, admission and financial aid officers, and others." Seems like a good choice considering both authoritativeness and bias. How about the Cato Institute? There is a Wiki entry for this one, too, which describes Cato as "an American libertarian think tank headquartered in Washington, D.C." whose mission is "to originate, disseminate, and increase understanding of public policies based on the principles of individual liberty, limited government, free markets, and peace." A think tank report lists it among the nation's top think tanks (although it isn't clear what this measures). Cato is clearly a known entity, but given its that its mission is based on "limited government," it's safe to assume a strong bias in favor of home schooling.

Wikipedia isn't the only option for checking on sources. Your sociology professors will know about the reputation of most journals in the field. And don't forget librarians. Not only do they know the reputations of lots of sources, they can show you reference guides that discuss hundreds if not thousands of sources. Ask them about *Magazines for Libraries*—a wonderful but underused resource.

Interrogating Sources: An Example Reference List

Here is a reference list from a sociology paper on gender inequality. If this were our student's work, how would we judge the choices this student made? Let's consider each source:

1. The Gender Inequality Index (2010). Retrieved November 16, 2010, from http://hdr.undp.org/en/statistics/gii/
2. Gender and society (2007). Retrieved November 16, 2010, from http://www.trinity.edu/~mkearl/gender.html
3. 10 extreme examples of gender inequality (2009). Retrieved November 16, 2010, from http://listverse.com/2008/11/20/10-extreme-examples-of-gender-inequality/
4. The natural basis for gender inequality (2008). Retrieved November 16, 2010, from http://scienceblogs.com/gregladen/2008/12/the_natural_basis_for_gender_i.php
5. Gender inequality: women under stress (2009). Retrieved November 16, 2010, from http://health.howstuffworks.com/wellness/stress-management/women-under-stress.htm
6. Gender inequality begins at 16 (2006). Retrieved November 16, 2010, from http://www.hrmguide.co.uk/diversity/occupational-segregation.htm

Source #1 is a United Nations website for Human Development Reports. This seems like a good source for such information, doesn't it? In fact, the citation doesn't do it justice. It *should* have included not just the title of the page but also the organization that hosts the site. If "United Nations" had been there in the reference list, we would likely have been satisfied with just a quick glance at the citation because we're familiar with that organization. Thumbs up for the source. Thumbs down for the citation.

How about source #2? A quick look at the page shows it's actually a *student* project from Trinity University in San Antonio Texas. We don't know anything about the student who wrote it, but if she were already an authority on gender and society she probably wouldn't have done this project for a course assignment. Thumbs down!

Reference #3 is a rather odd site—just random lists of things. In addition to the list of gender inequality examples cited, we find "Top 10 Evil Serial Killers" and "10 Bizarre Discoveries From the World of Batman." Not exactly scholarly stuff. And can we even trust that the people making these lists are experts in those topics? A little bit of digging around the site takes us beyond skeptical to outright cynical:

> Listverse was built on the efforts of readers just like you. Readers who didn't have any experience as writers but decided to put a list together and send it in. So here is the deal: we will pay you $100 for your efforts. You don't need to be an expert—you just need to have great English, a sense of humor, and a love for things unusual or interesting.

Four thumbs down. (And besides, their standards for "great English" don't even include proper punctuation.)

Source #4 is a little trickier. It's a "science blog," but the blog is not hosted by an organization we're familiar with. Not compelling. Source #5 is on the "How Stuff Works" website and it's impossible to tell who writes these articles. This might be a fine source for answers to questions like "Are Kevlar mountain bike tires worth the cost?" or to figure out "How to Unclog a Toilet Without a Plunger." But as a source for a scholarly paper? Nope.

Finally, #6: This one came close to being a winner. The "About" page of the website gives us little useful information—only that "HRM Guide is an independent online publisher of articles and information about Human Resource Management and related subjects." We also learn that advertising "is accepted on (almost) all HRM Guide website pages." Not much to go on there. However, at the top of the cited page we find this:

A report by the Equal Opportunities Commission (EOC) shows that gender inequality in education and work begins at sixteen. Girls and boys study most subjects in roughly equal numbers for GCSE. Girls do very well but once their examinations are over the genders rapidly move towards traditionally "male" or "female" subjects.

Now, the EOC *does* show up on Wikipedia, from which we learn it was "an independent non-departmental public body in the United Kingdom, which tackled sex discrimination and promoted gender equality." Too bad the paper didn't cite the EOC report instead. That *would* have been an excellent choice.

CITING SOURCES AND AVOIDING PLAGIARISM

8

In Chapter 7 we discussed how to choose sources and use them effectively. You also need to know why, where, and how to cite your sources. This means learning the conventions for citing sources within the text and constructing the list of references at the end. We cover these things in this chapter.

Why to Cite

Sociologists cite sources for many reasons. You are likely familiar with two: avoiding plagiarism and giving others credit for their work. But you probably haven't learned much about the equally important *intellectual and rhetorical* reasons for citing. Even if there were no legal or ethical issues involved, sociologists would still cite sources. Lots of them.

These other uses for citation involve rhetorical strategies— using sources in ways that develop our ideas and arguments clearly and effectively. Sociologists cite statistics from authoritative sources so readers will accept them. They cite research papers to justify their choice of methods or to show how their ideas or data add something new. And they cite because sociology, like all sciences, is a giant, slow-motion, crowd-sourcing activity. To have their work taken seriously, researchers must explain new findings in relation to what was done before.

Why to Cite

- *Legal:* To avoid committing plagiarism
- *Ethical:* To give credit where it's due
- *Rhetorical:*
  - To add credibility
  - To build on the work of others
  - To compare with the work of others

Where to Cite

Some kinds of writing, like magazine articles and newspaper reports, don't have lists of sources at the end. Authors of these genres must include any needed information about their sources within the text itself. In contrast, most academic papers and many types of professional writing include complete citations in a reference list at the end. For these kinds of writing authors include brief "in-text" citations within the paper pointing readers to specific sources in the reference list.

Novice writers often assume that the in-text stuff is the simple part. After all, reference lists have such detailed and varied requirements for punctuation, volume and issue numbers, editions, and so on. But experienced writers see it differently. Once you learn the mechanics, making a reference list is like doing a paint-by-numbers picture: you have to get some details right, but there's not much thinking involved. In contrast, there are many options for in-text citation. Do you put citations at the end of the referenced material or somewhere else? Do you include page numbers? The authors' names? The title of the paper or book? The name of the publication or organization? Some of these decisions are determined by the citation style. Others follow conventions of the discipline. Yet others are rhetorical choices—decisions you make about which details will be relevant or compelling for readers at that moment. Given the number of options, it's not surprising that students are often confused about where to place in-text citations and what to include.

For sociology, the convention for *where* you put the in-text citation depends in part on *how* you are using the cited material. Sociologists typically place in-text references in one of two places: directly after the referenced material is announced (especially if the authors are explicitly invoked by name) or at the end of the cited material. The categories in the "Ways to Use Sources" section of Chapter 7 (pp. 148–155) are useful here. Although there is certainly some randomness in practice, this is a typical pattern:

- If you are using the source as *Background*—place the citation information at the end of the cited material.
- If you are using a source as an *Argument, Theory*, or *Methods* source—refer to the authors directly in the text by name, placing the citation information just after the name(s).

Here are some examples.

Background Source (cite after material from that source):

With increasing urbanization and industrialization, hiring decisions based on particularistic criteria (e.g., race) cannot be easily sustained, given the demands of a modern economy for highly skilled labor (**Hogan and Featherman 1977**).

Argument and Theory Source (cite with date directly after author names):

My focus on racial differences in employment hardship is appropriate for at least two reasons. First, the unemployment rate has been criticized as a measure of labor force performance. . . For instance, in a study of four southern rural counties, **Rungeling et al. (1977)** found that unemployment rates were consistently very low (about 3 percent), while "subemployment" affected over 40 percent of the work force. For the same period, **Levitan and Taggart (1973)** reported national levels of subemployment of about 11.5 percent. Clearly, the unemployment rate minimizes both the absolute and relative extent of all employment-related hardship in the nonmetropolitan South.

Methods Source (cite directly after author names):

As described in the next section, **the Labor Utilization Framework (LUF) of Clogg and Sullivan (Clogg 1979; Clogg and Sullivan 1983; Sullivan 1978)** provides a useful analytical device for addressing several objectives on changing black employment-related. . .

The next example shows a combination of in-text citations typical for sociology research reports. Note also how the author combines summary, paraphrase and direct quotation.

It is difficult to forecast future patterns of racial homophily. A well-documented literature on cross-race friendship dyads and networks among adolescents and the school-aged population (**Goodreau et al. 2009; Wimmer and Lewis 2010**) provides little hard evidence on temporal or life cycle changes in racial homophily. Racial differences in homophily are nevertheless large. For example, **McPherson et al. (2001) showed** that whites have more racially homogeneous networks than do other racial and ethnic groups. **Smith (1999) similarly reported** that only 6 % of whites and 15 % of blacks had a close friend of another race ...

Kao and Joyner (2006:972), in fact, provided evidence of "an overwhelming preference for same-ethnic peers over same-race (different-ethnic) and different-race peers." They also demonstrated that interracial friendships increase in number when opportunities ...

ASA Tips for In-Text Citation

In the How to Cite section that follows, we describe the nuts and bolts of using the ASA (American Sociological Associations) style. But while we're on the topic of in-text citations, here are a few things to look out for when citing in ASA style.

If you name the author or publishing organization in the text, **don't** repeat it in the citation.

NOT THIS: **Rungeling et al. (Rungeling 1977)** found that unemployment rates were consistently very low ...
BUT THIS: **Rungeling et al. (1977)** found that unemployment rates were consistently very low ...

When giving an overview of research literature, you will sometimes include multiple citations in the same sentence. If you have different sources for each subtopic or factor, it's important for readers to know which material came from which source. Place each citation at the end of the material relevant to that source, **not** all piled up at the end.

NOT THIS: Moreover, drinking and dating portend the risks and rewards of the transition to adulthood. Early and frequent alcohol use, in particular, is a risk factor for many health and adjustment outcomes, including adult alcoholism, sexual risk-taking, depression, violence, and lowered educational attainment (**Bonomo et al. 2004; Hingson et al. 2003; Windle and Davies 1999; Felson, Teasdale, and Burchfield 2008; Staff et al. 2008**).

BUT THIS: Moreover, drinking and dating portend the risks and rewards of the transition to adulthood. Early and frequent alcohol use, in particular, is a risk factor for many health and adjustment outcomes, including adult alcoholism (**Bonomo et al. 2004**), sexual risk-taking (**Hingson et al. 2003**), depression (**Windle and Davies 1999**), violence (**Felson, Teasdale, and Burchfield 2008**), and lowered educational attainment (**Staff et al. 2008**).

If you reference two works by the same author in the same sentence, include the name only once.

NOT THIS: Drawing on social learning theory, network science, **Granovetter (1973) and Granovetter (1983),** we argue that romantic partners likely function as network bridges...

BUT THIS: Drawing on social learning theory, network science, and **Granovetter's** seminal work (**1973, 1983**), we argue that romantic partners likely function as network bridges...

For block quotes (longer passages identified by indentation rather than quotation marks) you can place the citation before or after the block. Here's an example of the former (note date and page number in parentheses):

This is also exemplified in a conversation between three boys in an English class that was documented by **Morris (2008:738):**

> Kevin: "I don't want to put in a lot of extra effort like that. I'll just do the basic stuff and get a B." "I got an 87 in here," he says proudly. Warren chimes in, "Yeah, I hate these pussies who make like an A minus and then they whine about it." Kevin says, "Yeah it's like why do you care? Why does it have to be better? Nothin' wrong with a normal grade!"

Although ethnographic studies have documented substantial within-gender diversity in the construction of gender identities, the evidence . . .

Another option is to include the source name and date before the block and put only the page number at the end of the quotation. This is a good choice if you want to make sure your readers are aware of the source as they read the quotation. In this example, the General Accounting Office would be considered an authoritative source, so the authors chose to invoke the organization by name prior to the quote to frame how readers would think about the quotation:

Most organs transplanted in the United States come from cadaveric donors. A report from the **General Accounting Office (1993)** describes the process:

> Organ donation is dependent on voluntarism and generosity as well as solicitation and decision-making at a time when family members are under the stress of bereavement. . . . If the family consents to donation, OPO staff coordinate the remainder of the procurement

activities, including recovering and preserving the organs and arranging for their transport. (**Pp. 17–18**)

Finally, if you do not mention the source explicitly before the block, place all citation information *within* the block at the end of the quote:

> A classic study of "class structure and conformity" is a paradigmatic example of how an individual's open-minded attitudes are the consequence of that same individual's education and occupational self-direction.
>
> Members of different social classes, by virtue of enjoying (or suffering) different conditions of life, come to see the world differently—to develop different conceptions of social reality, different aspirations and hopes and fears, different 'conceptions of the desirable' (**Kohn 1969:7**).

How to Cite

To this point in the chapter we've discussed why and where to cite. Here we address the nuts and bolts of documenting sources, which basically involves making your citations look like they should.

The different ways of formatting citations are called "styles" (which is confusing because they're really more like formats). The most important (and perhaps most annoying) thing to know about citation styles is that different disciplines often use different styles. When you began your first year of college, you might have thought that MLA (Modern Language Association) style was *the* formatting style. After all, it's usually the only form taught in secondary schools—at least in the United States. But if you look at the tens of thousands of books and articles published by scholars in all disciplines each year, most of them do *not* use MLA.

Tip: Don't Wait Until the Final Draft to List Your Sources

Students often think that citing sources is a trivial part of writing . . . just some tidying up to be done at the last minute. There are two problems with this. One is that you may be setting yourself up for accusations of plagiarism: "Yes, Professor, it is true that I paraphrased that part from one of my sources . . . But I was planning on citing it later. *Really* I was." The other is that it hides an important part of your work from those who are offering you guidance along the way. If your instructor (or someone else giving you feedback) cannot see the sources you are using, how can they tell you whether they are appropriate or compelling?

Although it's fine to hold off until near the end to properly format your citations, include at least placeholder citations as you go. One way to do this is to insert a unique identifier such as [Ref AAA] at the appropriate place within the text, and include a shorthand citation for that identifier at the end (a Web address is perfect if one exists), like this:

AAA: http://www.asanet.org/abcde/.pdf

The American Sociology Association, the official organization of sociologists in the United States, has its own style, called ASA. It's the style your sociology professors are most likely to require, so we cover it in some detail here. But be aware that some sociology journals and publishers use other systems and your professors may prefer those. The journal *Social Forces* uses the Chicago style, while *Journal of Marriage and Family*, a multidisciplinary journal, uses a modified form of the APA style. Make sure you know what each of your professors expects. If your professor doesn't specify a style, choose one of the major social science styles and use it consistently. For social science assignments, don't use a humanities style (especially ones that use footnotes instead of reference lists and use Latin terms like "ibid" and "op. cit."), but APA or Chicago would work, too. Almost every college library now has online guides to the major styles.

Tip: Use a Citation Management System

Back when we were in college, we had to learn all of the details for every style we were required to use. But you have computer applications that can do this for you; they're called citation management systems. They can output your reference lists in any style you choose and get all of those italics and colons right. As we are writing this, some of the most popular systems are Zotero, RefWorks, Endnote, and Mendeley. Your library probably supports at least one. Be smart—ask a librarian to help you get started with one now, and you'll save yourself much time and hassle for the rest of your educational life.

A Brief Guide to ASA Style

Social science citation styles have two parts: (1) in-text citations—how you identify sources within the paper, and (2) a reference list at the end that includes all the sources you consulted. We'll explain both parts.

ASA In-Text Citation

Most of your citations will be articles or scholarly books. For ASA, you must include the last name of the authors and the year of publication. The following table tells you how to handle most citation situations.

The Situation	What to Do	Example
If the sentence doesn't otherwise include the authors' names...	put them in parentheses, along with the date.	The constraints of finances and available partners may lead lower income adults to marry later in the life course or not at all (Edin 2005).
If you have already mentioned the author by name...	the parentheses should only include the date.	In her theories regarding women's life choices, Gerson (1985) pointed out that choices are all made in the context of women's social conditions...
If there are **two** authors...	use "and" between the last names.	Identifying liaisons thus provides an attractive means of understanding how substance use behaviors may be transmitted within low-density or highly clustered friendship networks (Henry and Kobus 2007).

The Situation	What to Do	Example
If there are **three** authors ...	the *first* time you cite this source, include each author's last name.	Scholars, however, have noted that having a child together often creates lasting ties between parents whether or not they remain romantically involved (Roy, Buckmiller, and McDowell 2008).
	After the first time, use the shorthand "et al." (for "and others").	Evidence also indicates, however, that fathers have a great social interest in their children (Roy et al. 2008).
If there are **four or more** authors ...	use "et al." every time.	(as above)
If you are referencing more than one source at the same time ...	separate the information for each source by a semicolon.	Explanations for behavioral similarity require disentangling effects of peer selection (i.e., homophily) from peer influence (McPherson, Smith-Lovin, and Cook 2001; Valente et al. 2004).

The Situation	What to Do	Example
If you are quoting or discussing a specific page or set of pages . . .	include page numbers after the date with a colon in between (no spaces).	Regarding his baby daughter, one father said it was important to "be a part of her everyday living . . . at least for the first year or whatever" (Reed 2006:123).

ASA Reference List

Entries in ASA are listed alphabetically by author last name. For entries authored by individuals rather than organizations, include first and last names unless only initials are listed in the source. For the first or only author, put the last name first. For subsequent authors, keep the first name first. (Don't blame us. We didn't make this stuff up.)

Each type of source has its own format. Here are common cases, but see the ASA website or your school's library site for complete details.

The format for books:

Author1 (last name inverted), Author2 (including full surname, last name is not inverted), and Author3. Year of publication. *Name of Publication* (italicized). Publisher's city and state (or name of country if a foreign publisher): Publisher's Name.

The format for journal articles:

Author1 (Last name inverted), Author2 (including full surname, last name is not inverted), and Author3. Year of publication. "Title of Article." *Name of Publication* (italicized)

Volume Number (Issue Number): Page numbers of article.

Source Type	Reference List Example
book	Wilson, William J. 1990. *The Truly Disadvantaged: The Inner City, the Underclass, and Public Policy.* Chicago: University of Chicago Press.
journal article/ periodical	Felson, Richard, Brent Teasdale, and Keri Burchfield. 2008. "The Influence of Being Under the Influence: Alcohol Effects on Adolescent Violence." *Journal of Research in Crime and Delinquency* 45(2): 119–41.
authored by organizations	National Longitudinal Study of Adolescent Health. 2001. *Network Variables Codebook.* Chapel Hill: University of North Carolina.
website	US Department of Justice, Bureau of Justice Statistics 2014. "Data Collection: National Crime Victimization Survey." Retrieved December 19, 2014 (http://www.bjs.gov/ index.cfm?ty=pbdetail&iid=4905).

We're sure that you will quickly run into a situation not covered here. Look on the Web for a solution. But if you follow even these basic rules, you'll produce a paper that will strike your professor as scholarly and serious. You don't want to be random about these practices because it looks careless.

Some Special Situations

At some point you will likely need to cite sources that don't fall into the categories we have reviewed. Here are answers to some common questions.

What If the Source Doesn't Have an Author?
This is often the case for publications produced by government or nonprofit agencies or corporations. In that case, the organization name takes the place of the authors' names.

Do I Need to Include Page Numbers?
Only if you are quoting or closely paraphrasing, or if you are discussing material from a specific part of the book. For the in-text citation, include the relevant pages number(s) directly after the date.

When Should I Use a Block Quotation?
For ASA, use blocks for any quotations more than four lines long. Single-space and indent the entire block. Do <u>not</u> use quotation marks, too! Quotes of four lines or less should be placed within the text using the regular margins, set off by quotation marks.

What if the information or idea came from someone I communicated with directly rather than a published source?
Acknowledge the source in a <u>footnote</u> like this:

> Personal communication with Yvonne Haddad, Professor of History and Islamic Studies at Georgetown University.

Citing Stuff From the Web

Until very recently, the material we cited was printed on physical paper—with pages . . . and page numbers. Citation formats still reflect that past, even though more and more paper documents are being digitized and newly published material often exists only on the Web. This can cause some confusion. Here are a couple of things to keep in mind:

In Print and Online

At this time, many books and most scholarly articles coexist in the paper and digital worlds. If a print version exists, it is usually proper to use the print-version citation (with volume numbers, page numbers, and so on). Even though you most likely read a journal article online, we still think of the paper version as the *real* one. We generally cite such things just as if they were paper—except that we add information at the end of the citation stating where and when we accessed it online.

Web Pages as Sources
Non-scholarly sources increasingly exist only as websites. Standard citation elements such as titles, publishers, page numbers, and even authors either don't exist in the traditional sense or they aren't clearly indicated. Because citing Web pages is both common and a common source of confusion, let's take a closer look at how to do this in ASA. The basic principles are to make clear both what the hosting organization is <u>and</u> which specific Web page(s) you are referring to.

In-Text Citation

✓ **Don't** put the URL within the text, only in the reference list.

✓ **Do** cite the sources within the text just like a printed source: (author or organization name, date)

Reference List

✓ **Don't** use a URL <u>in place</u> of a citation in the reference list. The URL is only part of what is required.

✓ **Do** include the URL along with the date you looked at the page— <u>following</u> the other citation information, like this: Retrieved <date> (URL)

✓ **Don't** use *only* the name of the organization or only the title of the page as a citation.

✓ **Do** include the identity of the organization <u>and</u> the title of the specific page in the reference list.

Tip: Don't Include Names of Library Databases in Your Reference List

When students find an article using a library database, they often include the database name—Socindex, JSTOR, Web of Science, and so on—in the citation. Don't—at least don't when using ASA style. A library database is merely a tool for locating sources; it doesn't have any connection to the authors or play a role in the publishing process. Say you need to cite an article from *American Sociological Review.* You happened to find the article through a link from JSTOR, but you could just as well have gotten there via SAGE. Or a professor could have emailed you the citation or a link to the article. Your readers don't care how you found it. They just need the citation.

Avoiding Plagiarism

Why is our discussion of plagiarism in the Sources chapter? Because when students who *are not* intentionally cheating get into this sort of trouble, it is usually because they aren't using or citing sources appropriately.

Avoid Patchwriting

"Patchwriting" describes the kind of pseudo-writing in which big chunks of quoted or closely paraphrased text are "stitched" together with little bits of the student's own writing. Your professors recognize this for what it usually is: last-minute attempts to complete a paper using sources students haven't truly understood—and possibly not really read. Patchwriting is not only poor writing; it can get you into trouble.

Here's why: When you use large chunks of other people's writing just to make your paper longer, you have two choices and they are both bad: One is to clearly cite all of that undigested material—showing your teacher that you really haven't done much writing (or thinking) of your own. The other is to cite minimally, being intentionally unclear about what came from the source and what is your own work; this deception could be interpreted as plagiarism, even if you include a few citations. The best way to avoid patchwriting is to start working well ahead of the deadline, take good notes, and build your paper around your own ideas. See the Style chapter for more about how to do this well.

Patchwriting

Besides outright cheating (and you know what that is), the most common cause of plagiarism trouble occurs when students do *patchwriting* (also called *patchwork writing*). Patchwriting gets its name from the way students "stitch" together chunks of text written by others—doing little of the actual writing themselves. This might show up in an assigned paper in a sociological theory course as unnecessarily long quotes from Durkheim, Marx, and Weber texts, or in a library research paper with long, strung-together passages from sociological research reports. Or it might manifest in taking large blocks of text from a source, changing a few words (sometimes including an in-text citation, sometimes not) and passing that off as adequate paraphrase (it's not). Whatever the specifics, you're doing patchwriting if most of your paper consists of quotation and paraphrase of what other people have written with relatively few thoughts or ideas of your own.

Because patchwriting is so common, it's worth thinking about the reasons students do it. It may be that you don't believe you know enough to offer your own thoughts on the topic and therefore defer almost entirely to the experts. This is especially likely if you grew up in a culture with writing conventions or values that differ from Western academic norms. Or perhaps you haven't yet mastered the techniques of reusing other people's work—quoting, paraphrasing, and summarizing—needed for successful sociological writing. (For the basics, see Chapter 7: Choosing and Using Sources.)

And there's another possibility: procrastination. Having put off writing that sociology paper for weeks, you are now short on time and you know too little about the material. So you scramble to find passages from your sources that seem at least relevant to the topic. The assignment requires a minimum of ten pages and you have barely two pages worth of ideas, so the longer the quotation or paraphrase the better—right? As a result, there's little of *you* in your paper. If you're accused of plagiarism for turning in such a paper, you might well deserve it. Even though you didn't turn in a paper literally written by someone else, it's not really your own writing either. (If you were judging a furniture design competition, would you accept a chair assembled from an Ikea kit?)

No one can write a good college-level paper of more than a page or so the night before it is due. Putting yourself in that situation can lead you to make really, really bad choices. Your school probably has an office of academic support. Those folks can help you do better in your classes in many ways, including time management. It's free. Use it. Really.

When Is Plagiarism Not Really Plagiarism?

You have likely figured out by now that academic writing is not one specific genre. Literature professors write different kinds of papers and assign different kinds of writing than do their colleagues in physics. Neither looks much like what your sociology professors publish or ask their students to produce. But here's something you might not know: There are also important differences in what counts as plagiarism.

Although it's a bit of an oversimplification, it's useful to think about kinds of scholarly writing as lying on a spectrum between "essays" and "reports." Essayists think of their writing as works of art as well as scholarship. They strive for originally in expression as well as in ideas, and they expect the same of their colleagues and students. When a humanities professor asks you to write an "essay," that's the world you're in. In contrast, those in the sciences—including sociology—generally see their writing mainly as a vehicle for communicating ideas and findings. They often refer to "reporting" or "writing up" their work. These scholars do care about their writing, with a focus on being as clear and concise as possible, but they don't have the same sense of writing as an artistic product. Because of this different attitude toward prose, writers of reports sometimes reuse small bits of previously publish material. This is called *text recycling.*

Text Recycling

Although essayists would scoff at the idea of reusing chunks of prose from their prior published work in a new essay, report writers often see the practice as a matter of sensible efficiency and useful consistency. For example, say the sampling procedure you used in your most recent research project is nearly identical to the procedure you used in a previous study. Why write an entirely new description of the procedure when you could easily adapt the one you wrote for the earlier work?

Here are some things you should know about *text recycling* for your sociology courses. First, sociology spans a wider range of research and writing practices than almost any other discipline. Some of your sociology assignments will require essay-like writing (e.g., ethnographies or experience essays); other assignments, especially in medical, business, or psychological subfields, may require something similar to reports in some medical journals. Regardless of whether recycling is permitted in the latter, it is very unlikely to be acceptable in the former.

Second, text recycling in sociology is acceptable in only a few specific situations. Here are the most common:

- From grant proposals to research reports: If research is funded through a grant, material written for the grant proposal will often be reused when reporting on the research once it has been conducted.
- In Introduction sections: An author writing a paper building on her own prior research might adapt material from a prior paper of her own (or by her research group) explaining the purpose of a study or reviewing the literature.
- In Methods sections: Technical descriptions of databases, sampling techniques, or statistical methods might be recycled from one's own previous papers or from organizations whose resources you are using, such as surveys or databases.

But even in the situations described here, verbatim recycling only makes sense if the language in question is the best possible choice for *your* context—which is different from the rhetorical context of the source. For example, the website for a database you are using may describe the sampling procedure in great detail, but this doesn't mean *your* readers need all that information or will understand the technical terms used in the original.

Especially in the school context, decisions about recycling should always be made carefully and judiciously. Although *text recycling* is accepted practice in some professional writing situations, it likely runs counter to your school's honor code and therefore could be construed as plagiarism. If you believe that recycling a particular passage is your best option as a writer, ask your instructor or mentor whether recycling that material is permissible and a good writerly choice.

If you choose to recycle material in a paper you are writing for a course, we strongly urge you to make it very clear to your instructor exactly which material in your paper is recycled. Here is a good procedure:

- Highlight all recycled passages in gray. (Gray shows up on printed copies.)
- For each passage, include a footnote (1) stating that the highlighted material has been reproduced from elsewhere and (2) citing the sources, including the page number.

Following this practice helps protect you from charges of plagiarism. It also provides an opportunity for your instructor to help you learn the nuances of recycling in their area of specialization.

Textual Gifts

There is one other way in which sociologists may legitimately use the language of others without attribution. And unlike text recycling, this one applies across academia. Almost everyone who writes professionally has learned the value of getting feedback from trusted colleagues. Before submitting an important piece of writing—whether grant proposal, research report, or book manuscript—most sociologists will ask others for honest and constructive feedback on their work.

Among the various issues mentioned in this feedback, some comments may suggest alternative wording for short phrases or even entire sentences. The suggested text might be more understandable than the writer's original prose or perhaps it avoids undesirable associations which the writer hadn't considered. We might call such freely offered material *textual gifts.*

Those who accept such textual gifts typically don't acknowledge the specific text in any way. The gifted material isn't put in quotation marks or cited. The one exception is if a particular bit of suggested prose ends up being important to the work in some way—perhaps as a key phrase or metaphor. In this case, the author may thank the colleague in a note of acknowledgment, but it has to be a very important contribution to deserve such special treatment. You are telling your reader that this word or phrase was an "ah-hah" way of thinking about the topic for you.

Depending on the aims of the assignment and your professors' own preferences, you might be encouraged to get feedback on drafts or be explicitly prohibited from doing so. If the latter—well, there you go, no gifts for you. If the former, check with your professor so you know what is and isn't allowed when getting feedback on your work in progress.

STYLE

9

"OK, Dr. Bach, *you* tell the students they should *never* use first person."

"Oh yeah! I'll even say that using "I" or "we" is just plain *wrong*! . . . Because, uhm, . . . because it shouldn't matter *who* did the research!"

"Perfect! Then on the following day Dr. Burton will tell them that they *must* use first person, because . . . let's see . . ."

"I've got it: Because using "I" acknowledges that their observations are . . . hold on, I can't stop laughing! . . . their observations are subjective, clearly influenced by their own . . . uhm . . . experiences and biases."

"Oh, Linda, that's too funny!"

"I never get tired of this."

You may occasionally get the sneaking suspicion that your sociology professors are playing rhetorical tricks on you. But there are more plausible reasons why the conventions of sociology writing might seem capricious. One is that these conventions change over time. Another is that writers are simply inconsistent when there is no clear advantage or preference among the possible options. But here is the main reason: Many stylistic conventions, including those for voice and person, depend on context . . . and we professors often neglect to tell our students that our guidance applies only for certain situations. It certainly doesn't help matters that some well-intentioned but misinformed people have written books and authored Web pages stating "rules" for these things—as if they were simple matters that could be learned once and applied the same way everywhere. (Why don't these self-appointed rule makers *look* at some real papers from the last 50 years to see how they're actually written?)

So you have good reason to be confused, if not downright suspicious. We can easily imagine students are having conversations like this:

"Dr. Burton . . . Is she the one that doesn't like first person?"

"No, that's Professor Bail. I'm pretty sure Dr. Burton *likes* first person."

"Yeah, that's right about Burton. But Bail, he's just nuts! He wrote comments on one part of my paper telling me that it should be in past tense. And then, in another section, he edited a bunch of my past-tense verbs to make them *present* tense!"

Some of your sociology professors probably *are* crazy, but we hope this chapter will help you understand typical stylistic variation as a function of context rather than the whims of your instructors. We'll also offer some guidance on how to construct clear and effective prose.

First Person: I, We, My, Our

The use of first-person pronouns in sociology writing is complicated. Let's begin with an important distinction: Are you doing (a) a type of writing that sociological researchers produce, such as a research report or proposal, or (b) a type of writing done mainly by students for class assignments like those we discuss in Chapter 2?

If your assignment is in the latter category, your decisions about first person should follow any preferences your professor has stated. Aside from those, base your use of first person on how central you, the author, are to the writing project. For assignments centering on discussion and analysis of what *others* have written (using a case to illustrate a theory, for example), you're not so much a character in the story but the narrator. In these cases, refrain from using first person except when identifying your own ideas, claims, or interpretations. In contrast, more extensive use of first person is appropriate for genres in which you are writing about yourself—such as internship reports and papers using personal experience to illustrate a concept. In fact, doing these kinds of writing without first person would be awkward.

First Person in Scholarly Research Writing

For sociological research genres, things are rather more complicated. Use of first person tends to follow complex conventions that depend on structure (where the usage occurs in a paper) and rhetorical aim (what the authors are trying to do at that moment).

Figuring Out Your Professor's Preferences on First Person

Preferences for using first person is somewhat generational: The gray and wrinkled professor emeritus will likely favor much less use of first person than the fresh-faced professor with a new PhD. If you're not sure about your instructor's preferences, ask (as politely as possible) which of the following categories best fits his or her expectations:

> *Old School*: prefers sparse use of first person as described later for Introduction, Results, and Discussion sections. Rarely if ever uses first person in Methods.
>
> *Middle of the Road*: comfortable with moderate use of first person; same as for Old School but more of it—plus perhaps a bit in Methods, too.
>
> *Interpretive and Introspective*: allied with sensibilities of cultural anthropology; promotes more extensive use of first person (but perhaps still limited in the Results section).

You might also read some of your professor's own published work to see the choices he or she makes. You'll learn something and earn brownie points, too.

And if that weren't enough, these conventions also depend on the authors' stance regarding subjectivity. Sociologists who use qualitative methods are trying to capture, in rich detail, the nature of human social interaction in all its complexity. Because these methods require them to interact with and observe their subjects directly, these researchers understand that subjectivity is inherent in their work. Say two talented researchers each interview a dozen adult children of divorced parents. They will both learn something of value, yet because their conversations are shaped by their individual experiences, interests, and personalities, we don't expect them to learn *exactly* the same things. Sociologists who use qualitative methods, therefore, often emphasize this subjectivity by intentionally using first person frequently in their writing.

In contrast, sociologists who use *quantitative* methods tend to see subjectivity as undesirable even if unavoidable. Despite the inherent challenges of studying human subjects, these sociologists try to gather data that are reproducible and influenced as little as possible by the researchers themselves. Ideally, other sociologists could repeat their procedures precisely and obtain results that (while not identical because of random variation) would support the same conclusions. This adversarial relationship with subjectivity tends to correlate with more restrained use of first person.

With all of this complexity, you might be inclined to just avoid the use of first person altogether. That would be a mistake. In fact, the less frequently a sociologist uses first person, the more certain you can be that statements that *do* include it are among the most important in the paper. That's how scholars tend to articulate their main conclusions, ideas, objectives, and so on. You should do the same.

Different Norms for Different Sections

For research reports, the conventions for using first person are different for each section. To help you navigate this maze, here are section-by-section tips.

Introductions

1. It depends on which rhetorical part of the introduction you are writing. In Chapter 5, pp. 86–95, we break down introductions for research papers in terms of four

standard "moves." For moves 1–3, sociologists use first person infrequently. But they almost always use first-person pronouns in move 4 when describing their aims and hypotheses—typically with verbs like these:

> I/we: consider; identify; use; argue; hypothesize; predict; examine; assess

Literature Review/Theory
Use of first person is often used to elaborate on move 4 from the introduction, describing in detail the aims and methods of the project in relation to prior research:

> *I/we:* examine; analyze; present; suggest; test these hypotheses using the case of; move beyond prior research by; rely on three distinct theoretical traditions; test several competing hypotheses about; also examine the possibility that; employ three waves of data from; tease out nuances related to; would expect to see differences based on

Less common is use of first person to articulate the scope of the project, either to explain what *is* covered ("We focus on…") or *not* covered ("We do not address the question of…").

Data/Methods
This section varies the most among sociologists: *Old-school* practitioners avoid first person in their Methods sections like the plague, while the *Interpretive and Introspective* crowd embraces it. Here are typical examples for the latter group:

> *Referring to data/sample—I/we:* include; divide our sample into; use data from; selected respondents with; restricted our sample to; count the number of; combined these responses

Referring to analysis—I/we: control for; code; assign; operationalize; categorize; estimate; include a dummy variable for; recoded these responses into; estimated variance using; restricted my analyses to; look at the independent effects of

Results

Of all sections, first person is used least often here. When it is, the authors are usually doing one of three things:

1. Making meta-comments about their analysis (what they did):

   I/we: further investigated; use logistic regressions to predict; included an interaction between

2. Providing organizational guidance for readers:

   We now turn to our analyses of; in each table, **we** begin with; **we** next examine; **we** first examine the roles of; next **we** turn to; **I** begin from

3. Noting a lack of (or limited) observed trends in some part of their data:

   I/we: find only one significant relationship between; find little evidence that; do not find; find no significant relationship between

Discussion

First person is almost always found here, usually for one of two purposes:

To announce or summarize your main findings:

I/we: have argued that; find that; suggest that; extend their research by; am inclined to believe that; hypothesized that; do not find strong evidence that

Or to describe limitations of your study:

I/we: are limited to analyzing; are limited by available data; have no information on; do not, however, have direct measures of;

    Although we: did our best to account for; control for

Abstracts

Because abstracts present the entire paper in miniature, use of first person here mimics the various sections described earlier.

I/we: suggest; analyze; conclude; use data from; posit; evaluate whether; find that

Active and Passive Voice

The issue of active versus passive voice must be one of the most misrepresented in all of writing education. Here's the dogma: "Always use the active voice; it makes your writing stronger/ more interesting/more lively." Here's the reality: Active voice *can* help with these things, but using *only* active voice results in awkward, cumbersome prose.

In active voice, somebody (or something) *does* some sort of action: <u>Milo hit</u> the ball. This gives agency to actions—we know who the doer is. In passive voice, some action is done *to* somebody (or thing): <u>Milo was hit</u> by the ball. We don't know *who* threw the ball at Milo. Maybe it just rolled off a table during an earthquake and Milo just happened to be on his hands and knees looking for his pencil. Passive voice is often a good choice if there are many or unnamed doers, or when the doers are unknown or irrelevant: <u>Max was elected</u> President of the United States is probably a better choice than <u>The people of the United States elected</u> Max president.

Mixing active and passive constructions allows us to connect sentences in ways that make paragraphs flow. Anyone who takes the trouble to look will see that expert sociologists commonly interweave active and passive constructions, shifting back and forth in a seamless fashion. In the following examples, we indicate **active voice with bold** and <u>passive with underlining</u>.

Within the last several decades, **social science and biomedical scholars vigorously explored** the impact of childhood health on morbidity in later life . . . <u>These explorations were frequently grounded</u> in the conceptual and empirical literature on cumulative disadvantage, <u>a body of research that also experienced exponential growth</u> in recent years.

So forget the dogma. Figure out what fits best at each point in your paper. Here are some examples showing common ways sociologists use both active and passive voice:

Describing Prior Research

If a single study is being introduced, active voice is likely used:

For instance, in a study involving interviews with a large sample of adolescents, **Giordano, Manning, and Longmore (2006) find that** romantic relationships provide some of the same rewards and are characterized by some of the same dynamics as friendships.

On the other hand, if a trend or consensus in prior research is being established (many doers), passive voice is likely:

Low birth weight <u>has consistently been related to</u> poorer health from childhood through adulthood, illustrating the powerful influence of early life health on lifelong health.

Having health problems before the age of 10 <u>has been associated with</u> a greater likelihood of having diabetes at age 50 years and older.

Describing Data

Figures and tables might be referenced in either active or passive voice (even in the same paragraph):

Figure 1 illustrates the logic of weak ties and network bridges with three simple graphs.

<u>As shown in Table 1</u>, gender and racial variations in these school outcomes were in keeping with prevailing patterns. . . . **Table 1 also shows** self-reported athletic involvement.

Statistical tests might also be described either way:

<u>One-way analysis of variance tests were performed</u> to test the significance of gender and race differences in reported grades and school misconduct.

We used one-way analysis of variance to test the significance of gender and race differences in reported grades and school misconduct.

The dogma: Passive voice is something to be avoided whenever possible.

The reality: The best sociological writing involves frequent shifts between active and passive voice. Active is often more lively and engaging, but without passive in the mix, writing becomes long-winded and disjointed.

Coherence: Being a Trusty Guide

It's January and you are back for the spring semester. Alex, a good friend from your hometown, just transferred to your school and, to your good luck, was assigned to your dorm, where you've been living since August. The weather on the first day of classes is awful—38 degrees and raining hard. Alex opens the door and steps outside, on the way to the chemistry building, where you both have your first class of the day. You pull him back inside, saying, "Follow me. I know a route that stays inside almost the whole way." You lead Alex through a virtual maze of stairways, hallways, back doors, and tunnels. In a few minutes you arrive in the basement of the chemistry building, warm and dry. "Wow," says Alex, "that was awesome! But I have no idea how we got here or how to get back that way." "Huh," you reply. "I never thought about how complicated this was for someone who hasn't been around here much." The next day you lead Alex again, but this time you take a moment at each juncture to show Alex some directional cues: As you leave the first hallway, you say, "First we're going to the other end of our dorm. . . . Now look behind you; remember that yellow sign on the door we just came out for the way back. . . . Now we need to go to the tunnel that takes us under Marshall Street, so we'll take the stairs to the basement—it's through this door marked 'Rooms 001–056.'" It doesn't take much longer than it did before, but now Alex can see how each step connects to the previous one. He'll understand where he's headed next and be able to make sense of the route.

Your readers need you to guide them in a similar way. You are well acquainted with the ideas and sources in your paper, but your readers are likely in unfamiliar territory. To help them understand where you are taking them (rather than just dragging them along behind you), point out the landmarks at each junction—whether you are stepping from paragraph to paragraph or leaping from section to section. The bigger the jump, the more detailed the directions readers need. The more turns there are along the way, the more useful it is to describe the path before you set out.

Units of Discourse

Students often think about structure only in terms of topic sentences and paragraphs. But to write effectively, you need more sophisticated concepts. The "topic sentence" oversimplifies how good writers actually begin paragraphs. And for papers longer than a couple of pages, you need to think not only about paragraphs but also sections and subsections. We're going to take you from the novice world of paragraphs and topic sentences to the expert concepts of *units of discourse*.

Most sociological texts are built from multiple-paragraph chunks. Each chunk has its own task. In books, the largest chunks are chapters. In research papers, the largest chunks are the major sections—Introduction, Methods, and so on—each with its own heading. In longer or more complex papers, these sections may be further divided into labeled subsections. But such chunks also exist in texts that are more essay-like, except that there are no clear markers showing where one chunk ends and the next begins. Writers of essays need to take special care to help their readers recognize the chunks and see how they are related.

Your campus likely has similar levels of organization. Here at Duke University, the largest-scale "sections" are East Campus, Central Campus, West Campus, and the Medical Center. West Campus is further divided into subsections: the "main quad," Keohane Quad, and so on. From the level of the quad we move down to individual buildings. These levels of hierarchy are essential to navigating the complex campus. If a visitor is on the main quad standing in front of the Sociology/Psychology building, it's easy to give him directions to another building on that quad: "The Allen building? It's the last one on the left as you're heading toward the Chapel." But if this visitor needs to get to the Carr building on East Campus, the directions will be longer and more complex (and involve a bus ride).

Let's step back now, and think about the "units" that make up a typical paper: Sentences are combined to make paragraphs, groups of paragraphs make up subsections, groups of subsections make sections, and sections make up the whole paper.

Unit Introductions: The Keys to Coherence

The concept of discourse units—paragraphs, subsections, sections—can help you understand how to guide your reader effectively through the different parts of your paper. Let's look at some examples to see how sociologists do it.

The text of Figure 9.1 comes from a research paper titled "Unnecessary Roughness? School Sports, Peer Networks, and Male Adolescent Violence" (Kreager 2007). We have included only the paragraph intros from the passage discussing the debate on the social role of youth sports. Because this passage begins a multiparagraph unit, the *first* paragraph has to do two introductions: It must first introduce this larger unit, which it does in the first sentence of the paragraph. The remainder of this paragraph focuses on the proponents' arguments; the *second* sentence of the paragraph does that intro work for that paragraph. Another way to think of this is that the first paragraph includes a one-sentence intro—but because it is starting a "subsection," an additional sentence is added at the beginning to introduce the subsection.

In looking at this first paragraph, we see how unit intros can help readers anticipate what's coming. But they can also show readers how what's coming next is connected to what they have read so far. Pointing readers back to prior material—the previous paragraph, section, or even the paper's introduction, depending on what makes most sense—helps readers make connections. It gives writing "flow."

To see how paragraph intros can link previous and upcoming material, look again at Figure 9.1—paying attention

The salience of athletics in adolescent culture fuels ongoing debates about the social role of youth sports. On the one hand, proponents have long argued that interscholastic athletics positively impact adolescent development . . .	*Section intro* ¶ 1 intro
Critical scholars, <u>however</u>, assail traditional views of youth sports as incomplete and problematic . . .	¶ 2 intro
Critical <u>feminist</u> scholars have taken particular interest in the relationship between sports and gendered violence. <u>Rejecting the view that sports help to curb antisocial behavior</u>, some researchers assert that the hypermasculine cultures characteristic of many contact sports teach violence as an acceptable means of maintaining valued male identities . . .	¶ 3 intro

FIGURE 9.1 Example of Introductions to Discourse Units.

to the underlined words and phrases. Unlike paragraph 1, paragraph 2 has only a single introduction to do, which is fulfilled with a single sentence. Note the use of <u>however</u> to point back to the prior paragraph (and signal contrast) while indicating what's coming next. The intro of paragraph 3 has two sentences: The first specifies a more specific group of critics— <u>feminist</u> scholars. The second begins with a clause that connects to prior ideas. Only after this do we see something that resembles a typical topic sentence, a statement of these critics' argument about masculinity and violence.

Let's look at another example from the "Unnecessary Roughness" article. Within the Theoretical Background section of this paper is a subsection labeled Social Control Perspectives. That's what comes just before the four-paragraph subsection shown in Figure 9.2 titled Social Learning Perspectives. The beginnings of each paragraph in this subsection

In contrast to social control theories, social learning perspectives allow for subgroup variation in attitudes toward violence and law violation. Accordingly, **individuals learn antisocial values and techniques within intimate social relations**, particularly among friends and family members [citations] ...	Points *back* to prior section First sentence continues to introduce the subsection topic: **social learning** Second sentence introduces **¶ topic: antisocial values within intimate relations.**
At the heart of social learning approaches is the idea that **delinquency**, like any other behavior, is learned in social interaction ...	Points *back* to subsection topic **¶ topic: delinquency**
Hughes and Coakley (1991) apply social learning ideas to the seeming paradox of **athlete deviance**. Rather than suggesting that athletes' antisocial behaviors result from social alienation or the rejection of cultural values, they contend that such behaviors stem directly from the normative definitions learned in sports, a concept they call "positive deviance." ...	Points *back* to subsection topic **¶ topic: athlete deviance**
Peer relationships play central roles in the learning process, particularly during the status-conscious adolescent years (Coleman 1961) ...	Points *back* to subsection topic **¶ topic: peer relationships**

FIGURE 9.2 Another Example of Effective Introductions to Discourse Units.

are shown on the left. Note how the intros to each of these paragraphs keep the parts clearly connected to the whole—pointing backward and **forward**.

Here is one last example of unit linking showing a nice variety of intro moves. This one comes from the Theoretical Background section of the article "Are Suicidal Behaviors Contagious in Adolescence? Using Longitudinal Data to Examine Suicide Suggestion" by Abrutyn and Muellera (2014). Following the first subsection, Suicide Suggestion and the Media, is another titled Suicide Suggestion Via Personal Role Models. Here are

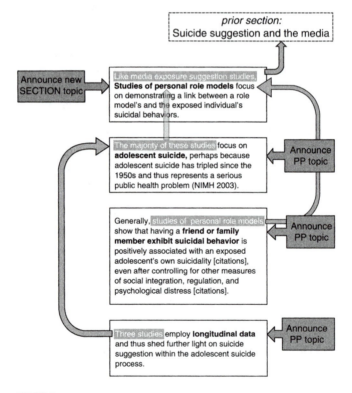

FIGURE 9.3

the introductions for each of the four paragraphs for this latter subsection (Fig. 9.3). We identify links to prior material with highlighting and **current (just beginning) topics in bold**.

As a reader, these introductory moves often go unnoticed, doing their work quietly. They're like street signs. When you know where you're going, you don't pay them any attention; but when you're unsure which way to go and you can't find any signs, you miss them. (Of course, misleading signs are worse than none at all, so be careful to get your intros right!)

Finding Your Structure

Getting ideas on the page is hard. So when we're drafting, it makes sense not to interrupt our thinking to figure out where things best belong. But students often don't realize that once most of the content is written, they need to go back and organize everything.

In Chapter 1 we told you about C. Wright Mills's suggestion to write major ideas onto notecards and then sort them into meaningful sequences. (Today we might print our drafts and cut them up instead.) You can try this technique to find a good structure for your material once you have a draft. The major piles are your sections. What's a good order for the piles? Make notes about what each pile contributes to the paper and how each relates to what's come before; that will help you figure out your section intros. Now do the same for the paragraphs that make up each section. As you write these section and paragraph intros, you're building the "you" into the paper. This is some of the most important stuff in your paper—right up there with your main question and the evidence you use to answer your question.

Writing Concisely

Here are two versions of a passage from an imaginary student paper:

Student A

According to Edward Kanopka and Joseph Pagani in their book *The Draw of Class Reunions Among Men and Women*, their results did not suggest a strong correlation between gender and whether people attend their high school reunions (Kanopka and Pagani 1981). Their data show that men and women choose to go to their reunions at about the same rate.

Student B

According to Kanopka and Pagani (1981), men and women do not differ in their patterns of attendance at high school reunions.

Which do *you* prefer? Given that your sociology professors have many papers from your class to read, which do you think they'd prefer reading? If you think your professor would be the least bit impressed by Student A, think again. This is what we would think: "This student clearly didn't spend enough time reading and thinking about this topic; he's adding lots of unnecessary words to the little bit of substance he has . . . hoping we won't notice." You want to be student B. Say what needs to be said; get rid of everything else.

To get to this level of economy, work from big to small. Don't waste time trimming words if you might end up cutting the whole sentence later. And don't mess around with sentences until you're sure the paragraph is a keeper.

Paragraph Triage

All effective writers learn to say goodbye, to speak a few kind words about a sickly paragraph, and then disconnect life support. When confronting a bloated paper, you might begin with triage: deciding which paragraphs are mostly fine, which can be saved with some work, and which need to be euthanized. Nothing you write should be longer than the idea justifies.

To do paragraph triage, start from the beginning of your draft and look carefully at each paragraph. In the margin (or with the "Insert Comment" feature) describe the *purpose* of the paragraph. Not just two or three words stating the "topic," but something that explains what the paragraph accomplishes, such as "Establishing the relevance of my topic" or "Specifying the dependent variables," or "Giving a contemporary example of Durkheim's sui generis."

Then decide what what's worth keeping:

1. Are there paragraphs that don't add anything of value to the paper? Print them out, fold them up, put them in a pile, and have a cremation ceremony.

2. What about stuff that seems useful but doesn't seem to fit where it is? If you can find a logical place for it, move it. If not, put it in a "holding tank" file. Once you've pared the document down to the good stuff, come back to this file and see where those pieces might work. For those chunks that don't find a good home, see step #1.

3. Are you covering the same ideas at different points in your paper? Decide which one works best. Then merge the others into that one—cutting anything redundant or irrelevant.

4. What if you feel confident that some of the material has value but you can't quite identify its purpose? Mark it with a question mark and see if it makes sense to add it to another paragraph. Sometimes a paragraph that isn't viable on its own can thrive with an organ donation. But be wary: If you combine paragraphs that don't logically

belong together, you will end up creating a monster—the dreaded *Frankengraph*.

Pruning Sentences

Imagine you are an arborist hired to manage a formal garden. As you take your first stroll through your new workplace, you see considerable potential. You admire the great variety of beautiful trees, wonderfully arranged in the landscape. But it's equally clear that the garden has not been well tended. Dead trees and branches disturb the views. In some areas, so many saplings have been left to grow that they are crowding each other out. It's hard to stay on the paths because of low branches that block your way.

What's your plan? To give the most promising trees enough air and light, you'll need to remove the dead ones and cut the dead limbs from healthy trees. And you mark many smaller branches for pruning—either to make a tree look better or to make it easier for visitors to walk the paths.

Your sociology paper is a garden. If you are like most of us—students and experts alike—your writing will need a good pruning before it's ready for the public. Before you open the gates for visitors, get out your tools and go to work.

Following is a paragraph from the Results section of a student's research paper. He had a good first draft with smart analysis. But now it was time for pruning. Before seeing what *we* have to say about the paragraph, take a look yourself. See if you can spot places that could benefit from a good trimming. Try reading the passage aloud. Your ears will often notice unnecessary repetitions that your eyes miss.

Two linear regression analyses were then conducted, one each for the subjects in the authoritarian and democratic priming conditions. For each of the conditions, the average difference in subject IAT response times between authoritarian and democratic adjectives was plotted against the affective distance between the subject's average self-identity and a different specific identity. For the authoritarian condition, the specific identify was "bigshot"; for the democratic, it was "workmate." Regression lines were fitted to each plot. Both regression analyses showed slight inverse relationships between response time difference and identity distance. The authoritarian condition gave an r^2 value of 0.041, which was not significant at the 0.1 level. For the democratic condition, the r^2 value was 0.115, which was significant at the 0.05 level.

There are good ideas here, but they're hard to follow amid the clutter. So what do we do? We'll start by using a technique that helps us better see what we've got: copying the passage into a separate document and then splitting it up into smaller units—sentences or even clauses.

1. Two linear regression analyses were then conducted,
2. one for the subjects in the authoritarian priming condition and the other for subjects in the democratic priming condition.
3. For the authoritarian priming condition,
4. the average difference in subject IAT response times between authoritarian adjectives and democratic adjectives was plotted against the affective distance between the subject's average self-identity and the "bigshot" identity.
5. A regression line was then fitted to the plot.
6. The regression analysis showed a slight inverse relationship between response time difference and identity distance, with an r^2 value of 0.041.

7. This relationship was not significant at the 0.1 level.
8. For the democratic priming condition,
9. the average difference in subject IAT response times between authoritarian versus democratic adjectives was plotted against the affective distance between the subject's average self-identity and the "workmate" identity.
10. A regression line was then fitted to the plot.
11. The regression analysis showed a slight inverse relationship between response time difference and identity distance, with an r^2 value of 0.115.
12. This relationship was significant at the 0.05 level.

As experienced trimmers of prose, we know it is foolish to start with the small stuff. Why carefully trim branches from a tree today if you're going to cut the whole tree down tomorrow? So we'll do this in two steps, looking first for big stuff that blocks our way or smothers good ideas (think chainsaw). Then we'll take care of the little stuff that's just unappealing (think clippers).

The split-up version reveals a lot of repetition. Lines 3 and 8 are almost identical—but the repetition here seems useful since the clauses are serving as signs along the path. In contrast, the repetition of lines 4 and 9 is not only annoying; it obscures important *differences*. The extra words make it hard to see what's different. Lines 5 and 10 are exact duplicates; surely that's not necessary. Now compare 6 and 7 with 11 and 12; the pairs are almost the same. These are good candidates for combining.

After some skillful use of the chainsaw, here's what we've got:

1. Two linear regression analyses were then conducted,
2. one for the subjects in the authoritarian priming condition and the other for subjects in the democratic priming condition.

3. For each of the conditions, the average difference in subject IAT response times between authoritarian adjectives and democratic adjectives was plotted against the affective distance between the subject's average self-identity and a different specific identity.
4. For the authoritarian priming condition, the specific identify was "bigshot"; for the democratic priming condition, the specific identify was "workmate."
5. Regression lines were fitted to each plot.
6. Both regression analyses showed slight inverse relationships between response time difference and identity distance.
7. The authoritarian priming condition gave an r^2 value of 0.041, which was not significant at the 0.1 level.
8. For the democratic priming condition, the r^2 value was 0.115, which was significant at the 0.05 level.

Now that we've done the heavy work, it's time for some delicate pruning. Let's see what we might want to work on next by highlighting repeated words and phrases.

1. Two linear regression analyses were then conducted, one for the **subjects in the authoritarian priming condition** and the other for **subjects in the democratic priming condition**.
2. For each of the conditions, the average difference in subject IAT response times between authoritarian **adjectives** and democratic **adjectives** was plotted against the affective distance between the subject's average self-identity and a different **specific identity**.
3. For the **authoritarian priming condition,** the **specific identify** was "bigshot"; for the **democratic priming condition**, the specific identify was "workmate."
4. Regression lines were fitted to each plot.

5. Both regression analyses showed slight inverse relationships between response time difference and identity distance.
6. The **authoritarian priming condition** gave an r^2 value of 0.041, which was not significant at the 0.1 level.
7. For the **democratic priming condition,** the r^2 value was 0.115, which was significant at the 0.05 level.

Too much repetition of the "priming condition" phrases—right? And the other repeated words could use some trimming, too. Once we've done that, it's time now to put the pieces back together and see what we've got.

Two linear regression analyses were then conducted, one each for the subjects in the authoritarian and democratic priming conditions. For each of the conditions, the average difference in subject IAT response times between authoritarian and democratic adjectives was plotted against the affective distance between the subject's average self-identity and a different specific identity. For the authoritarian condition, the specific identify was "bigshot"; for the democratic, it was "workmate." Regression lines were fitted to each plot. Both regression analyses showed slight inverse relationships between response time difference and identity distance. The authoritarian condition gave an r^2 value of 0.041, which was not significant at the 0.1 level. For the democratic, the r^2 value was 0.115, which was significant at the 0.05 level.

Much better, right? Our final step is to read through once more, cutting out individual words that don't do anything useful. Like this:

~~Two~~ linear regression analyses were ~~then~~ conducted ~~one each~~ for ~~both the subjects in~~ the authoritarian and democratic priming conditions. For each ~~of the~~ conditions, the average difference in ~~subject~~ IAT response . . .

And this:

~~Regression lines were fitted to each plot. Both~~ Regression analyses **for both conditions** showed slight inverse relationships between . . .

We end up with this:

Linear regression analyses were conducted for both the authoritarian and democratic priming conditions. For each condition, the average difference in subject IAT response times between authoritarian and democratic adjectives was plotted against the affective distance between subject's average self-identity and a different specific identity. For the authoritarian condition, the specific identify was "bigshot"; for the democratic, it was "workmate." Regression analyses for both conditions showed slight inverse relationships between response time difference and identity distance. The authoritarian condition gave an r^2 value of 0.0401, which was not significant at the 0.1 level. For the democratic condition, the r^2 value was 0.115, which was significant at the 0.05 level.

From 170 words down to 108. Nothing important was cut. What's left is easier to read.

Does writing concisely take time? You bet it does. And if you don't have a solid draft in hand well before the paper is due, you won't have time to do it. That's the difference between a paper with great potential and an excellent one.

Counterarguments, Concessions, and Limitations

Imagine you are head counselor at a new sleep-away camp for at-risk 11- to 14-year-olds. The camp owner asks you to investigate whether it's better to keep the boys and girls separate or have them do most of their activities together. You find two sources that discuss the issue:

A

At-risk adolescents act out when in large groups of peers of both sexes. This population seeks to gain status with others of their own sex by visible flirtation with the other sex, and to gain status with those of the other sex via acts of bravado and challenging authority. As a result, at-risk adolescents will behave better when isolated by sex.

B

At-risk adolescents exhibit complex behaviors when in large groups of peers of both sexes. The behavior of individuals is affected by self-perceptions of ranking among their same-sex peers as well as their histories within the juvenile justice system. Combining adolescents of both sexes may be advantageous in those activities that require . . .

Take a look at both. Which *type* of writing is more compelling: one that presents a simple, straightforward statement (A) or one that openly acknowledges complexity and uncertainty (B)? Most novices prefer the directness of the first to the seeming wishy-washiness of the second. But experts tend to be skeptical about overly simple claims, knowing that meaningful questions rarely have simple answers.

In addressing their more sophisticated audiences, sociologists will openly consider contrary points of view (***counterarguments***), admit the existence of plausible alternative interpretations or conflicting data (***concessions***), *and* acknowledge the **limitations** of their own research.

Novices often mistakenly believe that acknowledging counterarguments, concessions, or limitations *weakens* their arguments—thinking that readers will be more inclined to agree with them if they keep such information hidden. But for an audience of sociologists (including your professors), these elements can make your argument *more* compelling. Why? For one thing, they enhance your *ethos*—how your readers feel about you as an author. When you seriously address a counterargument, when you raise evidence that runs counter to your claim or explain how your claim doesn't hold for certain situations, when you state openly the ways in which your data are less than optimal, your readers get the sense that you're knowledgeable about your subject and that you're being straightforward with them. They can trust you.

Turning Weakness Into Strength

When you are seriously investigating an issue of substance, you will encounter ideas or evidence that casts doubt on your point of view. Students often think it's better to keep these things hidden. It might surprise you to know that professors think very highly of student work that accepts and addresses the real complexities of their arguments. In fact, processors often list students' *failure* to acknowledge counterarguments and contradictory evidence as among their most common disappointments with student writing.

So rather than sweep the limitations and logical conundrums of your paper under the rug, address them directly—like the pros do. Learn how to make counterarguments, concessions, and limitations work for you.

Also, scholarly audiences are reflexively skeptical readers. While they read, they think of objections—reasons why the author's claims might *not* hold. Now, if you happen to know that your professor always thinks out loud when he reads student papers, you might hide in his office closet. When he pauses to express an objection to something in your paper, jump out and explain why his objection doesn't negate your claim. But if hiding in a closet doesn't fit into your busy academic and social schedule, you'll have to resort to doing what experts do: anticipating such objections and responding to them in your paper.

Counterarguments and Concessions

Counterarguments are claims, reasons, or evidence that contradict the argument you are making. If you agree there is some legitimacy to a counterargument, we call it a concession—in that you *concede* the point. Either way, if you raise such a point, you'll want to follow it with a *response* explaining why it doesn't undermine your basic argument. The basic patterns are these:

Counterargument: So and so says X. **Response:** However, . . . [reason to dispute X]

Concession: We concede that Y is true. **Response:** Nonetheless, . . . [reason to disregard Y]

Here are published examples of each:

Men's cooking is leisurely, **some argue**, because they have more flexibility than women in terms of when and how often they cook (**e.g.,** Adler, 1981). . . . **But do** men who have significant cooking responsibilities and lose this flexibility find cooking less leisurely? **Not necessarily**: many of my	*counterargument* *response*

participants who had primary responsibility for cooking in their households still often experienced it as leisure.	
Two of the three temporal studies decomposed the weekly increase in men's time with children, finding that changes in men's behavioral propensities, not compositional changes in families, accounted for the increase. . . . **It may be true that** men's increased propensity to interact with children accounts for all of the temporal increase in shared time with children. . . . but this conclusion is based on analytic models employing relatively few controls.	*concession* *response*

Counterarguments are especially effective in theory-focused and essay-like genres. In research genres, we're more likely to find the close cousin of the counterargument: contradictory evidence. Concessions are effective in most genres; in research reports, they are found mostly in discussion sections.

Limitations

In sociological writing, acknowledgments of limitations are found mostly in one place, in one genre: the discussion section of research reports. If this makes you think they're not very important, you're wrong: They are an expected, and in fact essential, part of that section. Sociologists who fail to acknowledge the limitations of their studies would be considered by their colleagues to be either naïve or incompetent (and likely both). Here are typical examples of how it's done.

The idea of using data collected on an availability basis **presents challenges of bias and lack of representativeness. While we stress** the difficulty of collecting data in the study sites used by this research, **we concede that** a more representative sample of the residents of these countries would hold greater external validity. We therefore advise caution in applying these findings to . . .

There are obviously other factors which might influence the level of INR in any society . . . the health status of the society, . . . and the literacy rate. . . . **While it was not within the scope of this paper** to study such variables, **we feel that** such factors are important enough to be mentioned . . .

Though this study adds to the understanding of risky sexual behavior among adolescents, **it is not without its limitations. While** we use two waves of data to test our hypotheses, **we can only** measure friend characteristics during the first wave. Thus, our models cannot address how sexual activity or anticipation for future academic achievement affects network composition.

[T]**here are limitations to our findings. We had only one measure of** academic performance: teacher-awarded grades reported by parents. **We do not know whether these same** highly competitive students **would also** score highly on standardized tests or sustain such efforts on their academic achievement over time.

Deliberate, Don't Debate

In evaluating attempts to answer important or interesting questions, sociologists (including your professors) value attitudes of *deliberation* over *debate*. Trial lawyers debate; judges deliberate. Lawyers aim to win; judges try to make sound decisions based on careful evaluation of the evidence and circumstances. Although it's easier to adopt the lawyer's attitude, try to think and write like a judge.

Tricky Words and Phrases

> You keep using that word. I do not think it means what
> you think it means.
>
> —Inigo Montoya in *The Princess Bride*

There are some words that have meanings in sociology that are different from the everyday meanings you might associate with them. Using these words incorrectly make your writing seem amateurish . . . and they may annoy your instructor. (Hint: If you *want* to be an annoying student, there are easier ways—like texting in class.) To be fair, unless you read a lot of sociology, you can't know which words these are unless someone just comes right out and tells you. So we will.

Word	What It Doesn't Mean	What It Does Mean
significant	important	unlikely due to chance alone
associated	having to do with something	correlated: when one thing changes, the other changes, too
random	haphazard; arbitrary	all possible samples have an equal chance of being selected
society	the high status or wealthy	social structures in some bounded group
culture	high-brow things like opera	widely shared meanings, values, or practices
control	taking charge	studying the effect of changes in one thing while holding another thing constant

Phrases and Practices to Avoid

In addition to misusing certain words, students often bring to sociology classes several other writing habits that will not play well. Here's a short list. Ignore it at your own peril.

- Don't make vague, unsupported assertions about what people typically do or believe:

  > **Most people** in the United States . . .
  > **People have always** . . .
  > **In today's society** . . .

- Don't use "male" or "female" to refer to humans when you are talking exclusively about adults (men and women) or just about children (boys and girls):

  > **Males** are at the forefront of corporate success and power.

- Avoid stale metaphors and clichés:

  > There are certain barriers that limit a woman's ability to **climb the corporate ladder.**

- Don't invent "facts" or make unsupported assertions based on your hunches:

  > There are three different types of support that males and females can receive from colleagues: emotional, informational, and instrumental (Wallace 2013). **It would seem that woman give and receive more emotional support, whereas men receive informational support.**

- Don't state that there are more than one of something—and then mention only one example.

This holds true especially in industries, **such as finance**.

This theory applies to many family relationships, **such as brother and sister**.

- Don't include stuff that is obvious from the rest of the sentence:

  However, **when comparing males and females on this topic**, males were 26 percent more likely to socialize outside of the office than females.

Avoid "Prove"

In student papers, we often see a sentence that begins, "These results prove that . . . " You may think the word *prove* is a good choice for showing that evidence supports your claim, but if you use it in a sociology paper, you may find out otherwise. Your professors associate the word *proof* with deductive reasoning, which is common in mathematics and some branches of philosophy. But deductive reasoning is quite rare in sociology. It's mostly used in theoretical work. Because human social interaction is so complex, sociological claims rely on probabilistic evidence (testing statistical hypotheses) or inductive reasoning from observations. Such evidence can never be certain, only consistent with a theoretical (abstract) idea. Instead of the definitive *prove*, sociologists typically use hedges such as *suggest, indicate,* or *show*.

A FEW LAST THINGS

At the beginning of this book, we told you the story of Georg Simmel, one of the founders of sociology, whose first attempt at a PhD dissertation was rejected because his writing was so careless. Because software now catches so many mistakes, it's easy to get lazy about proofreading and final preparations. Given the work you've put into writing a first-rate paper (right?), you want your professor to grade it in a positive frame of mind. But despite good intentions, even the best teachers can get harried and a bit testy while working their way through big stacks of papers—especially when students haven't taken the trouble to do the little things that can make this work a bit easier.

There are some things you can do so *your* paper won't be one of those that make professors grit their teeth or roll their eyes—and these are things that a spell checker can't catch. Some have to do with the writing itself; others are about getting the proper kind of document or file in your teacher's hands. Before submitting your paper, check the following items.

Proofreading Tips

Once you've worked on a paper for a while, it becomes difficult to see what you *really* wrote (as opposed to what you wanted to write). Here are two tricks that can help you catch errors and other glitches:

- Have your computer read your paper to you. Most computers and tablets now have built-in software that will read text aloud. Working on a paragraph or two at a time, turn on the speech function, look *away* from the screen, and just listen. When you notice something weird—perhaps a missing or duplicated word or an excessively long and complicated sentence—pause the recording and fix it.
- Start from the end of the paper (or from the end of each section) and read the last sentence. Then the next to last and so on until you get to the beginning. Reading the paper backward like this takes each sentence out of context, which lets you pay more intention to the sentences themselves.

Writing Issues

Understand that even experienced writers can't check everything in a single pass. Double-check whether each of the following items is a potential issue with your paper. For the best results, read your paper through the paper multiple times, thinking about only one issue at a time.

> *Quotations*: We've already discussed the problems of excessive quotation. Read through your paper one last time, looking at every set of quotation marks or block quote. If it's a single word in quotes, is it really used in such a special way that you need to point it out to the reader? If it's a phrase, is it distinctive enough to need direct quotation, or would a paraphrase in your own words actually be better? If it's a longer passage, could the quoted portion be shorter and still capture the essential idea?

Paragraphing: Look at the length of your paragraphs. Are there many one- or two-sentence paragraphs? Could they be combined with something else without sacrificing coherence or emphasis? Do other paragraphs seem particularly long? If there is more than one thought worthy of its own paragraph, split it up. Look at the way each paragraph begins: Is there an introduction that clearly sets up what the paragraph accomplishes? If not, make a more explicit beginning highlighting your ideas or intentions.

Citations: You might think that your professor won't notice if references are missing, but if he sees something interesting in your paper and looks for the citation—and it isn't there—you are marked as a careless writer. So go through your paper and make a list of every citation in the text. Then look at your references section and make sure that there is a complete citation for each one. We'll bet you'll find a couple that aren't there—it's a common mistake. Now, go through the opposite way. Look at your list of references and check to see that each source in that list is cited at least once in the text. If there's a reference that you don't use, eliminate it. And make sure every citation is complete.

Formatting and File Naming

So your paper is written, revised, edited, and carefully proofread. You've done everything you can, right? Not quite. There are still some macro-level formatting issues to address. If your professor specifies a format, follow it slavishly. It's not a suggestion, it's a requirement. (If you are writing a master's thesis or dissertation, the formatting requirements will be elaborate.

Plan for 2 weeks just to get them sorted out.) If there are no format specifications, here are some tips to make your submission look sharp. You wouldn't wear jeans to a professional job interview if you really wanted the job; don't dress your formal paper like it's going to a basketball game.

- *Title page*: If your paper is more than a few pages, it should have a title page. Center the title in the top third or so of the page (see pp. 146–147 for how to write a good title). Below that put your name, perhaps your student ID number, your contact information (your email and perhaps your cell phone), the name of your institution, and the date. Skip a few lines and write:

  > This paper was completed in partial fulfillment of the requirements for (your course number and section), (your semester or quarter, year), under the direction of (the name of your professor or whomever supervised the assignment). All of the paper is my own work, except for quotations as indicated.

- *Recycled text*: If you recycled any text in the paper (see pp. 195–197), make sure to highlight it in gray and add this: "All material recycled from my own previous work is highlighted in gray." That will protect you from charges of plagiarism related to such reuse.
- *Acknowledgments*: If appropriate for the genre, consider including a note of acknowledgment at the bottom of the title page: "I would like to thank so-and-so for help with (whatever . . . library research or analyses or feedback on the writing)." Acknowledgments aren't usually required; but if a teaching assistant, a librarian, classmate, or a friend provided useful guidance or input, it's a classy touch to show this appreciation. (Note: you do *not* need to include your professor in this list; that's our job.)

- *Table of Contents*: Papers less than 20 or so pages don't usually have a table of contents. But it is typically required for theses, dissertations, and formal honors papers; other long papers might benefit from one, too. If you include a table of contents, it should come after the title page. In the list, include the Abstract, all chapters (and perhaps their major subheadings), list of references, and any appendices. If you were directed to put tables and figures at the end rather than within the text, include those, too.

- *Summaries/Abstracts*: If your assignment is a full-length research report or proposal, it should have some type of summary before the paper begins. At the top of the page, repeat the title. Then, depending on the genre, put the words "Abstract" (for a research report), "Project Summary" (for a proposal), or "Executive Summary" (for a case study or policy memo), followed by the appropriate summary. Fit this on a single page, if possible. The body of your paper should begin on the *next* page, starting with the title yet again, centered at the top. (That title better be good—right?)

- *Page numbers*: Make sure that your paper has page numbers so that your professor can refer to them when commenting or asking questions. (Let's hope that one of those questions isn't "Where is the reference for that Muckfang 2015 that you cited on page 4?" Or, "Why aren't the pages numbered?")

- *Electronic files*: Most papers are now submitted electronically. If that's the case for you, and if you were not given specific instructions, here's what we suggest:
  - Send *both* a word processor file (like Microsoft Word) *and* a PDF file. Sending the PDF will ensure that the paper will look to your professor exactly like it looked to you—no matter what software or computer your professor uses. This isn't a hypothetical issue; formatting often gets fouled up this way—especially figures, tables, and the like. On the other hand, word

processing files are typically easier for teachers to comment on, which is especially important for early drafts or for a project that might continue past the original submission. So send both.

- Make sure the actual filename clearly identifies both you and the project. Your professor will be getting papers from your entire class, and maybe other classes, too. A file name like "finalpaper" won't be very helpful. Having to open a bunch of files, rename them with the student's name, and save them isn't the way to create that relaxed, warm feeling you want to inspire in your reader. Here's a good convention for filenames: your-lastname_yourcourse_semester_project name.

That's all we've got for you. Write well.

GIVING PRESENTATIONS ABOUT YOUR ORIGINAL RESEARCH

Although this is a book about writing, students who do original research are often asked to give presentations on their research, too. Here are some tips to help you make the most of these opportunities. Whether you are presenting to your classmates or at a professional meeting, the same principles apply.

Keep to the Time Limit

No matter how good you think you are at predicting the length of your talk, you can only know how long it really is by rehearsing, for real, out loud. It's best to do this at least once in front of an audience (even if it's only your dog).

Give a Coherent Overview of Your Project

The fact that your fellow classmates may have heard about your project for weeks doesn't relieve you of the responsibility to start at the beginning. Allocate time to introduce your theoretical framework, describe your methods, present and discuss your findings, and wrap up.

- The "moves" that you make in setting up a talk are basically the same as those we discussed for writing introductions in Chapter 5. Introduce your topic and establish its importance, starting with the broad topic and moving quickly to your specific research question. Describe what the literature

says about it (very briefly), and note the gap in that literature. Pose your research question and describe how the evidence you will analyze helps fill that gap.
- After the introduction, describe your key results, answer
your question, and discuss implications of the answer.

Discuss the Literature—But Briefly

One major difference between papers and presentations is the
amount of space given to discussing literature and theory in
comparison with results and conclusions about them. Because
the field is so broad, most sociologists won't be familiar with the
literature relevant to your research question. Summarizing this
literature is a major part of sociological research writing, but it's
difficult (we could say boring) to do too much of this when
speaking. So in your talk, get to your results within the first
third of your talk, if not sooner. This means that in a 15-minute
presentation (typical for a professional meeting), you'd better
be talking evidence before 5 minutes is up. In a 45-minute presentation (about the longest you'll do, unless you get elected
president of something), don't pass the 15-minute mark without giving people something concrete from your analysis. In
that short first segment, you've got to introduce your topic, give
your audience a rough sense of the literature and theoretical
framework you are building on, define any key terms, pose your
question, and present any hypotheses that you've developed. It
sounds like a lot to do, but you'll be rewarded when you see
your audience perk up when you hit the first results.

Use Simple, Readable Slides

Most people use some type of visuals to aid their presentation
(e.g., PowerPoint or Prezi). The key is to keep it simple: The
text in the slides *and* what you say about them should be

much, much simpler than your written text. (We know one noted scholar who says that no slide should have more than nine words on it. That restriction might be a little extreme, but this fellow is a great speaker. You could do worse than to follow his lead.)

- The most important feature of visuals is that people should be able to *see* them. So make sure *everything* in every slide—every word, number, and variable—is large enough to be read by those in the back of the room. Major titles should probably be in at least 44-point type. Nothing should be less than 22-point type.
- Think about what your audience should be doing. If the slides contain too much information, they will be trying to read the slides and listen to you at the same time—doing neither very well.
- Every slide should do one of two things: either display information in visual form that you will discuss or provide signposts along the way. Your talk is an easy-to-digest description of the project; the visuals should guide your audience through the organization of what you are saying, aiding them in following your logical sequence, without being redundant with what you are saying.
- Preview any colors or other formatting in your presentation setting before your talk. Sometimes things that look great on your computer don't show up on a projection screen. Black on white (or a soft, light-colored background) is always a safe bet. Fancy things may be tempting, but simple black on white is actually easier to read.
- The rule about visibility is especially important in presenting your results. Leave out anything that the audience doesn't need to see at that moment. This means that you'll need to make new versions of figures and diagrams—stripping out everything but the key parts and making the fonts larger.

- Try to use figures and graphs whenever possible; they are more visually interesting and easier to take in than tables. Any visual should be clean, simple, and bold. Don't put up a table of hundreds of numbers, and say, "I know you can't read this, but . . . " If they can't read it, why did you put it up?
- If you want to present a table, it's often better to present just the few labels and numbers that are essential to your argument, and note the parts that you left out in passing (either in smaller print on the slide or in your talk). For example, if your key independent variables are race and gender, you might show just those two coefficients (clearly labeled, of course), and just note that you controlled for 10 other variables to make sure that your results weren't spurious.
- Avoid gimmicks like moving fonts and rotating transitions. Keep it simple and put your effort into the content and clarity of the presentation.

Don't Put Whole Sentences on Slides and Then Read Them Aloud

Nothing is more insulting to an audience than to have someone read slides to them that they could read much more quickly themselves. If you are nervous or afraid that you'll forget something important, you might want to write out your talk. But don't just paste parts of your paper; the talk should feel more like a TED talk than a written research paper. Use short, clear sentences (or even sentence fragments: sometimes this works verbally, when it wouldn't be acceptable in formal writing).

Speak More Slowly Than You Think You Need To

It's harder to follow complex ideas when they are spoken than when you are reading them because we can't pause the speaker to think along the way or scan back. Make sure to give the audience time to think about what you are saying. This is especially important when you present data, diagrams, or other complex material on a slide. Talk the audience through the slide and then just be quiet for a few seconds while they look at it.

Beginning and Ending

At the beginning have a nice, formal slide that has the title of your talk, your name and affiliation, and the venue (the meeting or class in which you are presenting) along with the date. Because presentations often get sent around just like papers, you'll want it to be identified as your work. Also, the title slide gives something to show while you are waiting to start. At the end, try to forecast to your audience that you are drawing to a close. You might have a summary slide that gives them the two or three main points that you want them to take away from your research report. You might end with suggestions for future research. In any case, warning your audience that you are about to end your talk gives them a chance to get ready to ask questions or applaud or do whatever comes next without leaving an awkward pause. To signal you are done, say something like, "Thank you for your attention."

If at all possible, find an opportunity to present your research to an audience before you finish writing your paper. This presentation is a great chance to organize your thoughts about the project. You will often discover the most important findings of your analysis when you think about what you want to highlight for other people. And we frequently figure out better ways to organize our material or highlight the most important ideas.

RESPONDING TO PROFESSIONAL PEER REVIEWS

If you submit a research report for publication in a real journal, experts in the field will review your paper, a process called *peer review*. But as a new researcher, those reviewing your paper aren't really your peers. These are people who have power over you. The guidance we offer here is intended mainly for those reviews you get from an editor and blind reviewers for a journal submission, but they apply to serious comments from professors who read your work, too.

Let's recognize first that this experience involves strong emotions. Writing is hard work, and it's a creative process, and one that often leaves us feeling vulnerable. Getting formal feedback on something into which you've put so much of yourself is unnerving. Unless the response to your work is "This manuscript is wonderful; it's absolutely perfect" (good luck with that!), you're going to be frustrated and disappointed . . . and possibly even depressed for a while. We suggest that you read over the reviews and the decision, then put these away for a few days until the emotions die down. Few of us can digest such comments when we are upset, and it's not a productive time to launch into work on your writing.

After you've settled down, read through the commentary looking for the broadest, most important suggestions for improving the work. At this stage, it is not useful to spend much time on the smaller editing suggestions that readers provide. After all, if you rewrite substantial parts of the paper, you might cut out entire sections that they comment on. Look for issues that strike to the structure of the argument, literature that you missed, suggestions for further analyses to eliminate alternative hypotheses, confusions about evidence, disputes about conclusions. These are the structural issues that determine whether or not a paper makes a contribution to the literature.

If there are major misunderstandings of what you were trying to accomplish with your paper, make note of those. It's tempting to be critical of the reviewers. How could they have missed the fact that you explained this matter in the last section, or the next section, or whatever . . . sloppy reviewer! Upon closer reflection, you'll realize that these people probably read your paper more carefully than almost any future reader would read a published version. So if they misunderstand you, that's your problem. It's *your* job as the writer to make sure your reader *can't* miss the point. In short, don't view your relationship with the reviewers as antagonistic. Attending to their criticisms will almost certainly improve your paper.

As a student, you are used to getting feedback from only one person of authority: your professors. Getting feedback from three or more can be confusing because they won't have the same opinion on everything. It's common for one reviewer to have serious concerns about one aspect of your paper and another reviewer not to mention that at all. Even more confusing is when reviewer a compliments something you did and another reviewer criticizes that same thing!

So you need to think about this strategically: If more than one reviewer criticizes some particular, substantial thing in your paper, then this has to be fixed. The only exception here is when the issue is something that would not be so important in another type of publication. In that case, this might be a clue that you sent your paper to the wrong place.

If two reviewers *disagree* about some point, look again to make sure it is a true disagreement. Often there is a problem with a paper, and reviewers suggest different ways out of it, or they express the problem in different ways. They are both trying to help you, and the problem is real. As the author, it's your decision about how to resolve the problem. But you ignore their signal at your own peril.

When you get a decision back from a journal editor, it will be a rejection, an "R&R" (revise and resubmit), or a conditional acceptance. If you are unsure what an editor's letter means with regard to these categories, be sure to ask a more senior person in the field: Editors at different journals sometimes use different language to communicate these things. (For example, some editors will say, "Unfortunately, we cannot accept the paper in its current form . . ." and then go on to say that they will entertain a revised manuscript: that's good news, believe it or not.)

Your response to the reviews should differ, depending on the decision. And not just in the difference between your angst-filled wails versus yips of joy. If the decision is a rejection, then read the reviews (after you simmer down), and look for major issues that are likely to hamper the paper's acceptability for other journals. Any big flaws of logic, evidence, or conclusions are unlikely to disappear through aging. You need to confront them straightforwardly, either by acknowledging them openly (if they can't be fixed), and arguing for a real contribution despite the problem, or by changing the paper to resolve the problems. A very common problem in papers is that the front end (introduction, literature review and theory) doesn't fit the back end (method, data and analysis). This mismatch often happens when a project evolves over time. You started out wanting to answer one question and thus fill a particular gap in the literature. But your evidence didn't quite live up to that task and pushed you over into a different analysis— which might be even more interesting than what you started out to do . . . but your writing and revision didn't keep up with these changes. If you've got this problem, you've got to fix it.

On the other hand, if a reviewer dismisses your paper for fundamental reasons with which you disagree (perhaps the reviewer is approaching the topic from a very different sociological perspective), then his or her comments may be irrelevant. You can hope not to get this reviewer, or someone from the same school of thought, again—but there is no way that you can change the paper to please this type of reviewer, so don't try. Address fixable problems, but don't be slavish about following advice at this point: This journal is not going to take your paper.

If you have achieved a "revise and resubmit" review, you are now on a path toward publication. Recognize that the editor has complete power in this situation. If she tells you that a reviewer's particular comment is important, it is *important*. Deal with it.

Every substantive issue raised by each reviewer should be addressed. We don't mean that you have to do everything that every reviewer says, but if you choose *not* to accept some advice because you are convinced that it is wrong, you will need to argue your point persuasively in a memo to the editorial team. Sometimes it is useful to address such misreadings in your paper directly, saying the equivalent of "Some people might think X, but . . . " where X is what the reviewer suggests. If it is going to be a common reaction to your paper, it's useful to tell the wider scholarly community why X is not a problem (or why you disagree with that argument).

After you have completed revisions to your paper and are ready for resubmission, make sure to read it as a whole once again (and hopefully have friendly colleagues do so as well). Sometimes piecemeal changes can ruin the flow of your text. You need to edit until it is a coherent product again.

Start writing your revision memo as soon as you begin revising. Begin with a list of bullet points that you will need to address one way or another. As you decide whether and how to address each concern, document your decision in the memo. As you make changes to the paper, take notes about what you have done to solve the problem raised. In the final version of the memo, begin by thanking the editor and reviewers for their helpful comments on your work, and then go through each person's issues in turn, showing how you have addressed them and giving page/line numbers in the manuscript where they can find those changes. Novices sometimes adopt a combative tone in this memo; their more senior colleagues are more likely to be respectful (if not bordering on obsequious). The truth is that these people are helping you improve your work toward publication—and they have the power to decide what gets published in that outlet. Be polite.

Here's a final piece of advice: Everyone gets rejected a lot. Our best journals have an acceptance rate in the single digits. Therefore, publication is a long, often frustrating process. Yet every article that you read in your literature search went through this process. And once you make it publication, your scholarship is out there for the duration, available for other people to read and build on with their own research. At that point, you have truly joined the scholarly conversation that we discussed in our first chapter. Welcome to our world.

REFERENCES

[Note: The first list includes those sources documented with in-text citations. For sources used as examples to illustrate writing strategies, see the second list.]

"Another Gay Parenting Study Finds Children Do Best With Mom and Dad; Will the Supreme Court Care?" Retrieved January 1, 2016 (http://www.christianpost.com/news/another-gay-parenting-study-finds-children-do-best-with-mom-and-dad-will-the-supreme-court-care-133939/).

"ASA Guide to Writing an Informative Abstract." Retrieved January 1, 2016 (http://www.asanet.org/journals/abstract.cfm).

Back, Les. "Take Your Reader There: Some Notes on Writing Qualitative Research." Retrieved January 1, 2016 (https://www.dur.ac.uk/writingacrossboundaries/writingonwriting/lesback/).

"Biography of Alejandro Portes." Retrieved December 31, 2015 (http://www.pnas.org/content/101/33/11917.full).

Bizup, Joseph. 2008. "BEAM: A Rhetorical Vocabulary for Teaching Research-Based Writing." *Rhetoric Review* 27(1): 72–86.

Borsari, Brian, and Kate B. Carey. 2001. "Peer Influences on College Drinking: A Review of Research." *Journal of Substance Abuse* 13: 391–424.

Brett, Paul. 1994. "The Results Section in Sociology Articles." *English for Specific Purposes* 13(1): 47–59.

Deegan, Mary Jo. 1988. *Jane Addams and the Men of the Chicago School, 1892–1918*. New Brunswick, NJ: Transaction Books.

Firestone, William A. 1987. "Meaning in Method: The Rhetoric of Quantitative and Qualitative Research." *Educational Researcher* 16(7): 16–21.

Goffman, Erving. 1979. *Gender Advertisements*. New York: Harper & Row.

Huang, Grace C. et al. 2014. "Peer Influences: The Impact of Online and Offline Friendship Networks on Adolescent Smoking and Alcohol Use." *Journal of Adolescent Health* 54(5): 508–14.

Knight, Louise W. 2005. *Citizen: Jane Addams and the Struggle for Democracy*. Chicago: University of Chicago Press.

Lambert, Tracy A., Arnold S. Kahn, and Kevin J. Apple. 2003. "Pluralistic Ignorance and Hooking Up." *The Journal of Sex Research* 40(2): 129–133.

Lehmann, Hartmut, and Guenther Roth, ed. 1993. *Weber's Protestant Ethic: Origins, Evidence, Contexts.* Washington, D.C.: German Historical Institute; New York: Cambridge University Press.

Lewis, David Levering, and Willis, Deborah. 2005. *A Small Nation of People: W. E. B. Du Bois and African American Portraits of Progress.* New York: HarperCollins.

McClintock, Elizabeth Aura. 2014. "Beauty and Status: The Illusion of Exchange in Partner Selection." *American Sociological Review* 79(4): 575–604.

"Men More Unsatisfied With Extra Chores in More Gender Equal Countries." Retrieved January 1, 2016 (http://phys.org/news/2015 -02-men-unsatisfied-extra-chores-gender.html).

Merton, Robert K. 1969. "Foreword to a Preface for an Introduction to a Prolegomenon to a Discourse on a Certain Subject." *American Sociologist* 4(2): 99.

Mills, C. Wright. 1959. "On Intellectual Craftsmanship." Appendix to *A Sociological Imagination,* pp. 195–226. Oxford: Oxford University Press.

Robinson, Keith, and Angel Harris. 2014. *Broken Compass: Parental Involvement with Children's Education.* Cambridge, MA: Harvard University Press.

Streib, Jessi. 2015. *The Power of the Past: Understanding Cross-Class Marriages.* New York: Oxford University Press.

Sullins, Donald Paul. 2014. "Child Emotional Problems in Non-Traditional Families." *SSRN Electronic Journal.* Retrieved December 2, 2015 (http://www.ssrn.com/abstract=2500537).

Swales, John M. 2011. *Aspects of Article Introductions.* Ann Arbor: University of Michigan Press.

"Using 'Pseudoscience' to Undermine Same-Sex Parents." Retrieved January 1, 2016 (http://www.theatlantic.com/politics/archive/2015/02/ using-pseudoscience-to-undermine-same-sex-parents/385604/).

Villarreal, Andrés. 2014. "Ethnic Identification and its Consequences for Measuring Inequality in Mexico." *American Sociological Review* 79: 775–806.

Wingfield, Adia Harvey. 2010. "Are Some Emotions Marked 'Whites Only'? Racialized Feeling Rules in Professional Workplaces." *Social Problems* 57(2): 251–68.

"Write and Get Paid." Retrieved January 1, 2016 (http://listverse.com /write-get-paid/).

Sources Used as Examples to Illustrate Writing Strategies

Abrutyn, Seth, and A. S. Mueller. 2014. "Are Suicidal Behaviors Contagious in Adolescence? Using Longitudinal Data to Examine Suicide Suggestion." *American Sociological Review* 79(2): 211–27.

Amato, Paul R., and Danelle D. DeBoer. 2001. "The Transmission of Marital Instability Across Generations: Relationship Skills or Commitment to Marriage?" *Journal of Marriage and Family* 63(4): 1038–51.

Bearman, Peter S., and James Moody. 2004. "Suicide and Friendships Among American Adolescents." *American Journal of Public Health* 94(1): 89–95.

Best, R. K. 2012. "Disease Politics and Medical Research Funding: Three Ways Advocacy Shapes Policy." *American Sociological Review* 77(5): 780–803.

Brown, T. H., Angela M. O'Rand, and D. E. Adkins. 2012. "Race-Ethnicity and Health Trajectories: Tests of Three Hypotheses across Multiple Groups and Health Outcomes." *Journal of Health and Social Behavior* 53(3): 359–77.

Burton, Linda M., and Lea Bromell. 2010. "Childhood Illness, Family Comorbidity, and Cumulative Disadvantage: An Ethnographic Treatise on Low-Income Mothers' Health in Later Life" *Annual Review of Gerontology and Geriatrics* 30(1): 233–65.

Chaves, Mark, Laura Stephens, and Joseph Galaskiewicz. 2004. "Does Government Funding Suppress Nonprofits' Political Activity?" *American Sociological Review* 69(2): 292–316.

Cort, Malcolm A. et al. 2009. "Education and Internalized Racism in Socio-Political Context: Zimbabwe and Swaziland." *The Social Science Journal* 46(4): 644–55.

Cross-Barnet, Caitlin, Andrew Cherlin, and Linda Burton. 2011. "Bound by Children: Intermittent Cohabitation and Living Together Apart." *Family Relations* 60(5): 633–47.

Eder, Donna. 1985. "The Cycle of Popularity: Interpersonal Relations Among Female Adolescents." *Sociology of Education* 58(3): 154.

Goldberg, Chad Alan. 2011. "The Jews, the Revolution, and the Old Regime in French Anti-Semitism and Durkheim's Sociology." *Sociological Theory* 29(4): 248–71.

Hamilton, L., C. Geist, and Brian Powell. 2011. "Marital Name Change as a Window Into Gender Attitudes." *Gender & Society* 25(2): 145–75.

Harnois, Catherine E., and Mosi Ifatunji. 2011. "Gendered Measures, Gendered Models: Toward an Intersectional Analysis of Interpersonal Racial Discrimination." *Ethnic and Racial Studies* 34(6): 1006–28.

Healy, Kieran. 2004. "Altruism as an Organizational Problem: The Case of Organ Procurement." *American Sociological Review* 69(3): 387–404.

Hippen, Benjamin. 2007. "Last Best Gifts: Altruism and the Market for Human Blood and Organs—by Kieran Healy." *American Journal of Transplantation* 7(1): 261–62.

Huang, Chien-Chung, and Wen-Jui Han. 2007. "Child Support Enforcement and Sexual Activity of Male Adolescents." *Journal of Marriage and Family* 69(3): 763–77.

Huang, Grace C. et al. 2014. "Peer Influences: The Impact of Online and Offline Friendship Networks on Adolescent Smoking and Alcohol Use." *Journal of Adolescent Health* 54(5): 508–14.

Kreager, D. A. 2007. "Unnecessary Roughness? School Sports, Peer Networks, and Male Adolescent Violence." *American Sociological Review* 72(5): 705–24.

Kreager, D. A., and D. L. Haynie. 2011. "Dangerous Liaisons? Dating and Drinking Diffusion in Adolescent Peer Networks." *American Sociological Review* 76(5): 737–63.

Leonard, Thomas C. 2005. "Protecting Family and Race. The Progressive Case for Regulating Women's Work." *American Journal of Economics and Sociology* 64(3): 757–91.

Lichter, Daniel T. 1989. "Race, Employment Hardship, and Inequality in the American Nonmetropolitan South." *American Sociological Review* 54(3): 436.

Lichter, Daniel T. 2013. "Integration or Fragmentation? Racial Diversity and the American Future." *Demography* 50(2): 359–91.

Longest, Kyle C., and Steve Vaisey. 2008. "Control or Conviction: Religion and Adolescent Initiation of Marijuana Use." *Journal of Drug Issues* 38(3): 689–715.

Maume, David J. 2011. "Reconsidering the Temporal Increase in Fathers' Time with Children." *Journal of Family and Economic Issues* 32(3): 411–23.

McCarthy, B., and T. Casey. 2008. "Love, Sex, and Crime: Adolescent Romantic Relationships and Offending." *American Sociological Review* 73(6): 944–69.

McCarthy, John D., Andrew Martin, and Clark McPhail. 2007. "Policing Disorderly Campus Protests and Convivial Gatherings: The Interaction of Threat, Social Organization, and First Amendment Guarantees." *Social Problems* 54(3): 274–96.

McPherson, Miller, Lynn Smith-Lovin, and James M. Cook. 2001. "Birds of a Feather: Homophily in Social Networks." *Annual Review of Sociology* 27(1): 415–44.

Miller, Kathleen E., Merrill J. Melnick, Grace M. Barnes, Michael P. Farrell, and Don Sabo. 2005. "Untangling the Links Among Athletic Involvement, Gender, Race, and Adolescent Academic Outcomes." *Sociology of Sport Journal* 22(2): 178–93.

Morris, E. W. 2008. "'Rednecks,' 'Rutters,' and 'Rithmetic: Social Class, Masculinity, and Schooling in a Rural Context." *Gender & Society* 22(6): 728–51.

O'Brien, T. L., and S. Noy. 2015. "Traditional, Modern, and Post-Secular Perspectives on Science and Religion in the United States." *American Sociological Review* 80(1): 92–115.

Read, Jen'nan Ghazal. 2007. "More of a Bridge Than a Gap: Gender Differences in Arab-American Political Engagement." *Social Science Quarterly* 88(5): 1072–91.

Robinson, Dawn T., Lynn Smith-Lovin, and Olga Tsoudis. 1994. "Heinous Crime or Unfortunate Accident? The Effects of Remorse on Responses to Mock Criminal Confessions." *Social Forces* 73(1): 175–90.

Schneider, Barbara Lynn, Gregory Wallsworth, and Iliya Gutin. 2014. "Family Experiences of Competition and Adolescent Performance: Competition and Adolescent Performance." *Journal of Marriage and Family* 76(3): 665–76.

Soller, Brian, and Dana L. Haynie. 2013. "Structuring the Future: Anticipated Life Events, Peer Networks, and Adolescent Sexual Behavior." *Sociological Inquiry* 83(4): 537–69.

Sykes, J., K. Kri, Kathryn Edin, and Sarah Halpern-Meekin. 2015. "Dignity and Dreams: What the Earned Income Tax Credit (EITC) Means to Low-Income Families." *American Sociological Review* 80(2): 243–67.

Szabo, Michele. 2013. "Foodwork or Foodplay? Men's Domestic Cooking, Privilege and Leisure." *Sociology* 47(4): 623–38.

Trinitapoli, Jenny, and Stephen Vaisey. 2009. "The Transformative Role of Religious Experience: The Case of Short-Term Missions." *Social Forces* 88(1): 121–46.

Tsoudis, Olga, and Lynn Smith-Lovin. 1998. "How Bad Was It? The Effects of Victim and Perpetrator Emotion on Responses to Criminal Court Vignettes." *Social Forces* 77(2): 695.

Umberson, Debra, Hui Liu, John Mirowsky, and Corinne Reczek. 2011. "Parenthood and Trajectories of Change in Body Weight over the Life Course." *Social Science & Medicine* 73(9): 1323–31.

CREDITS

Page 13, *Figure 1.4*: Pew Research Center/USA Today.

Page 133, *Figure 6.1*: From "Marital Name Change as a Window Into Gender Attitudes." *Gender & Society*, 2011.

Page 134, *Figure 6.2*: From "Gendered Measures, Gendered Models: Toward an Intersectional Analysis of Interpersonal Racial Discrimination." *Ethnic and Racial Studies*, 2011.

Page 135, *Figure 6.3*: From "Dangerous Liaisons? Dating and Drinking Diffusion in Adolescent Peer Networks." *American Sociological Review*, 2011.

Page 135, *Figure 6.4*: From "Dangerous Liaisons? Dating and Drinking Diffusion in Adolescent Peer Networks." *American Sociological Review*, 2011.

INDEX